Lord Mountmorres

The Danger of the Political Balance of Europe

Lord Mountmorres

The Danger of the Political Balance of Europe

ISBN/EAN: 9783743311145

Manufactured in Europe, USA, Canada, Australia, Japa

Cover: Foto ©ninafisch / pixelio.de

Manufactured and distributed by brebook publishing software (www.brebook.com)

Lord Mountmorres

The Danger of the Political Balance of Europe

THE DANGER

OF THE

POLITICAL BALANCE

OF

EUROPE,

TRANSLATED FROM THE FRENCH OF THE KING OF SWEDEN,

BY THE

Rt. Hon. Lord MOUNTMORRES.

Opininionum commenta delet Dies, veritatis judicia confirmat— Cic.

LONDON:

Printed for E. JEFFERY, PALL MALL.

M.DCC.XC.

TO

Lord Viscount TORRINGTON.

&c. &c. &c.

———

PERMIT me, my Lord, to address a translation of the Danger of the Political Balance of Europe to your Lord-

Lordship—and to hope that you will accept it as a tribute of private friendship, and as a mark of just regard and esteem, from a well-wisher to his country.

Examples of men who enter voluntarily and gratuitously into diplomatic employment are rare: neither are

are there many instances to be found of foreign ministers who discharge the duties of their offices with laborious application, unwearied diligence, private credit, and general satisfaction, in the countries from whence they are delegated, and to which they are deputed.

In considering your Lordship in that description of foreign ministers, I shall assuredly adopt an opinion from my own belief and conviction, from my observations during your long and constant residence at Brussels.— A general remark ought not to create particular offence: our embassies have not always

ways been filled with able men, which I have often regretted, in different parts of Europe.—The extent and sphere of compliment is limited, to men who consider it as one of the privileges of rank and independence to speak the truth.—Faithful copies of the portraits of Sir William Temple and the Count

Count D'Avaux, it is true, are not easily found; but a great country requires able ministers in foreign departments.

I have the honor to be,

Your Lordship's obedient,

Humble servant,

MOUNTMORRES.

London,
July 10, 1790.

PRELIMINARY.

THE spirit of the first works frequently evaporates in translations; as the essence of ether is often lost, when poured from one vial into another.——The Translator offers this work in an English dress, with a diffident hand, to to the impartial tribunal of the Public—If he shall have succeeded in representing the genius and capacity, which pervade the treatise on the Danger of the Political Balance of Power, he conceives that he shall have given satisfaction to the intelligent, information to the political, and amusement to the many.

In this work, the rapid progress of Russia, in somewhat more than half a century, from civilization to preponderance in the general system — the dethronement of Peter the Third — the accession of Catherine — the subjection of Courland — the appointment of a King of Poland, the nominee of Russia — the partition and dis-

dismemberment of that country — the Leonine convention with Frederick the Great, and with Austria—the Turkish wars—the policy of the Czarina — the interests of Denmark—the constitution, the character, the revolution, and present state of Sweden — above all, the agitation of the great question, of the consequences of the

the subjection of Turkey, and the establishment of Russia in the Mediterranean, and its importance to the maritime powers, are most happily displayed.

The idea of any state obtaining a general ascendant, may, or may not, be a chimera; but human affairs revolve in the same circle;
what

what has happened, may happen again; and novelty is but forgetfulnefs. Hiftory would be the amufement of children, and not the inftruction of men, if the paft did not prepare us for future events, and guide us through political mazes, with antecedent information.

The

The Russian troops have appeared with the greatest effects in the wars of Europe; Sweden and Russia have, at different periods, experienced their obstinacy in the battles of Pultowa, and of Kunersdorff.

With Russia we have had connections, treaties, and alliances, since the first intercourse

course with that country, in the time of Edward the Sixth. In a political view, little advantage has flowed from that connection; perhaps the only instance where she appeared on the political theatre in our favour, was at the close of the succession war, in 1747, when a body of Russian troops were on their march to counteract the effects

fects of German discipline in the French troops, and the victories of Saxe, and Lowendhal, in Flanders.

Our trade with Russia for naval stores, according to this work, produces a million of unfavourable balance against this country. By more accurate accounts from our

our own Custom-House books, eight hundred and twenty thousand pounds*.—Conjecture and accuracy combine to form a total, which it will be our policy to lessen, by producing these articles among ourselves. Contrary to that policy which obtained, with regard to

* Chalmers.

Ireland,

Ireland, in 1750, which cannot be here enlarged upon: the feed, the acorn of this great meafure, has been planted in Ireland this laſt feſſion, by a law to encourage the export of Iriſh fail cloth, a meaſure hitherto difcountenanced here, though it was recommended to the Britiſh Parliament, at the beginning of this century, by Lord Somers [*].

Prejudices there are, no doubt, against noble, and against royal, authors—envy exacts a compromise from men in exalted stations; flattering misconception and self-love have established

[*] Lords' Journal, vol. XVII. p. 485.

an opinion, that men who are above the rest of mankind in some, should be lower than the rest of their species in other, respects;—but fortuitous advantages do not alter the real character—fame and reputation are prizes which may be allotted to any description of men; and we must admire those who quit exalted stations

tions to enter into the common lift, who ftart in the popular race, and labour to gain the prize, by furpaffing mankind in the beaten tracks, and the common high roads of life.

Of royal authors the catalogue is fmall, though fplendid inftances occur in the annals of literature—The

arm

arm which wielded the moſt ſucceſsful ſword, directed a pen with ſimilar abilities:—the Commentaries of Cæ-ſar were dictated by the ſame ſpirit with which he fought. If an enlightened period was poſſeſſed of a ſage whoſe divine genius ranged through the immenſity of ſpace, revealed the myſteries of nature, and gave to time and to motion mathematical laws, the annals of the thirteenth century, the age of obscurity and darkness, record the science of Alphonsus the Wise, king of Arragon, the author of the Tables which bear his name; who cultivated philosophy and the abstract sciences upon a throne. — If Frederick the Great appeared the foremost character

character on the theatre of Europe, it is well known that he has eternized his fame in a posthumous work, dedicated to candour and to truth:—the prince who has surprised Europe with the eclat of his victories, with the courage of the twelfth Charles, without his temerity, will not lose reputation, upon an attentive perusal of this

this work; and the Public must be pleased with the production of a monarch, who appears to bring the genius of his great predecessor to appear once more upon the stage, and to revive the glories of Gustavus Adolphus.

CHAP. I.

INTRODUCTION—Ruffian Politics befre the Reign of Catherine the Second, from - - Page 1 to 19

CHAP. II.

Hiftory of Peter the Third and of Prince Iwan—Acceffion of Catherine, from Page 20 to 86

CHAP. III.

The Ufurpation of the Duchy of Courland, from - Page 87 to 102

CHAP. IV.

Affairs of Poland—Nomination of Staniflaus the Third by Ruffia, from Page 103 to 134

CHAP. V.

The Influence of the Ruffian Court in Denmark, from Page 135 to 143

CHAP.

CHAP. VI.
The Partition of Poland, from
Page 144 to 163

CHAP. VII.
Turkish Wars—Oriental System of Russia, from - - Page 164 to 206

CHAP. VIII.
Constitution — Russian Influence in Sweden — Affairs of Finland, from
Page 207 to 227

CHAP. IX.
Negotiations of England and Prussia with the Czarina—Interests of the Maritime Powers — The Importance of the Establishment of Russia, as a Naval Power, in the Mediterranean, from
Page 228 to 235

CHAP. X.
Conclusion — General Remarks — Summary of this Work, from
Page 236 to 255

THE DANGER OF THE POLITICAL BALANCE OF EUROPE.

CHAP. I.

Introduction.—Russian Politicks before the Reign of Catherine the Second.

A Kingdom, almost unknown in Europe during the last century, and gradually aggrandized at the expence of all her neighbours, whose civilization contributed only to make conquests, has menaced, for forty years the political balance of power:—Sweden, Poland, Turkey, Pruffia, and Germany, have experienced the effects of her enterprifing spirit;—all the courts of Europe had experienced her infolence before that tragedy, to which Catherine the Second, owed her elevation to the throne.

Since that period, from the Cafpian fea, to the ftreights of Gibraltar, there is no country of which Ruffia has not difturbed the tranquillity, or alarmed the precaution:

tion:—every year has produced new defigns, which arofe evidently from one general plan, and their execution has found no other obftacle, than that which has arifen from the revenues of that empire, which were often ftretched fo far, as to need a temporary repofe from the abufe of power, and the prodigality of government: but their exhaufted revenues, have not created the fecurity of other ftates; for, the hand of power, tired with the exertions of open violence, prepared for them a war not lefs dangerous, a war of negotiations:

ceasing to become the prey of the sword, they had still to encounter her artifices, her intrigues, and negotiations; the interior of that empire, presented a theatre of divisions, of trouble, and disorders, of which the springs and machines were fabricated at Petersburg; at length, after having excited power against power, and interest against interest, in the neighbouring states, the Empress of Russia predominated alone in that vast anarchy, dictated laws through her Ambassadors, and

prevented

prevented all the combinations of resistance.

This portrait is engraved, from a faithful representation of the last twenty years history of the North, and of the Levant.—Europe has seen at one time, the Ottoman Porte menaced with an invasion, of which Asia herself, could not limit the consequences; her tributaries corrupted, her allies bribed, or intimidated, the Crimea enslaved, Sweden under the yoke of a faction, subservient to Russia, faction discomfited without being altogether subdued, and reviving by the same protection which has plunged that kingdom, into a universal decline; Poland equally punished from the defects of her constitution, devoured by Russian troops, enslaved, dismembered, treated in every light as a Russian province; Courland reduced to the lowest state; the Council of Denmark governed by the same influence; Prussia insulated in the midst of two vast empires, whose masqued batteries could play, on the first alarm, upon the great Protector of the

the Germanic liberties; the rest of Europe, tranquil and indifferent, acting the part of a spectator, but not that of an arbiter.

In this crisis, the Ottoman Porte tired of buying peace with vast concessions, which enabled her enemies to compel her to make farther purchases, was roused from her lethargy, and her example awakened other powers, who participated secretly in her just resentment; each of them, was anxious, and engaged in the hope, or apprehension, of what they had to gain, or to lose in this conflict, in which a moiety of Europe was engaged; and from Italy, to the verge of the Baltic, this great question was discussed: —*what would be the consequence of a war, which would spread its baneful effects, in limitting the overbearing power of Russia?* — Where facts speak, a chain of reasoning is useless: history is here alone the torch of precaution — from the operation of the same causes, the same effects are produced; the events which have passed, prepare us for those which are to come; and

and hence the solution of the problem of the consequences of the present war, demands the examination, of this original question:— *what have been the permanent principles of the Russian Court, and their effects upon the reign of the Second Catherine?*

To resolve this question, we must reject the sophisms of inconsiderate politicians, and the allegations of manifestos; truth here reposes upon public notoriety.— Let us examine the chain of consequences; the examination will lead

lead us to conclusions, upon the due stability of the balance of power, which must affect these powers, who are most inattentive to their own interests.

In the period of the middle of the reign of Lewis the Fourteenth, those who had heard of the name of Russia, annexed no other idea to it, than that which is connected with a description of Tartars and of Cossacks;—but when a man of more energy than genius, formed to govern more by the impulse of his passions,

than

than by the slow empire of reason, a succesful warrior and a tyrannic legislator, had raised up this vast Colossus, which had been buried in a barbarous obscurity, they sprung at once, to a station of preponderance, and of power before Europe could well recognise their character.

This new empire entered rapidly into the general system, and immediately announced their predominating designs, with forces, proportioned to their extensive ambition:—at their head appeared a desa despot, absolute master of the eighth part of the habitable globe, of opulent mines, of a hundred provinces, whose natives were inured to all extremities of rigors of climate, of hunger, of want; warlike from the savage habits of their laws; disciplined by the severe pressure of despotism; insensible of fear as they were insensible of misery; obstinate in combat; strangers to fear and to desertion; calculated for conquest and destruction, more than for defensive war; and substituting fanaticism, for emulation and patriotism:—such

such were the people whom Peter the Great collected from the north of Europe, and from the northern limits of Germany, when he founded the capital of his empire at Petersburg.

From that period the views, and exertions, of Russia were enlarged; they were no longer bounded by incursions into the Asiatic countries: mistress of a marine in the Baltic, her influence was an interesting concern to all the maritime powers; her numerous and warlike armies could

could easily invade Poland, Sweden, Denmark; desolate that part of those states which should oppose her, and second the efforts of their enemies: from thence issues the necessary influence of the Court of Petersburg among the southern, and western powers, who may engage in the hostilities of the North, or of Germany; assuredly the most penetrating politician could hardly believe, at the peace of Newstadt, in 1721, that twenty-five years afterwards, a king of France should give the daughter of the

first

first Peter, the title of the Mediatress of Europe, that a Russian army, should approach the Rhine at the requisition of England, and that, in the subsequent wars, the Russians should pillage the capital of Brandenburg.

From the same causes the alliance of this court, was solicited according to exigencies: the other extremity of Europe ambitioned her alliance, and there were few political interests in which Russia might not engage, since they weighed so considerably in the political

political system of the neighbouring states, and in the general balance of Europe.

To these they united the advantage of being seldom liable to act upon the defensive, to find weak states placed as feeble barriers between them, and the neighbouring powers, states either poor or divided: by evading the laws of nations, she could master these obstacles, and carry on her operations at a great distance from home.

Her

Her forces, her position, promised an ascendant in negotiations, and her security gave a hardy boldness, in her arrangements with other states: treaties became subordinate to her interests, her allies were changed every ten years, and no court formed the same coalition, of haughtiness, and of artifice.

The last years of the first Elizabeth, substantiated that danger with which the liberties of Germany, and of the whole North, were menaced; an alliance which resembled a conspiracy, was secretly formed by the Czarina, and the houses of Austria and Saxony, against the King of Prussia; France engaged in this confederacy, and penetrated into the western, while Russia invaded the northern, parts of Germany:— governed by the same faction, which annihilated the royal authority, and which shed the blood of the most illustrious of her families, Sweden, straying from her true interests, united herself with her natural enemies, and attacked Prussian Pomerania; while Russia

Ruffia invaded that kingdom.—It would be eafy to foretel what would have been the confequences, had they not been prevented by the genius of that hero whom they afpired to fubdue, and by the event which placed the third Peter, on the throne of his Aunt.

CHAP. II.

History of Peter the Third—and of Prince Iwan—Accession of Catherine the Second.

THIS Prince, who for some time, was only known in Europe, through the medium of the calumnies of his assassins — this Prince, born and educated in Germany, had all the inclinations of his native country, and a contempt for his new subjects. — Master of Holstein, a member consequently

consequently of the German Empire, he added weight to the Russian Crown, interfered in the German system, in his own personal right, and fortified his influence with new alliances with the northern powers. Happily, this prospect did not inspire him with ambition; he was influenced only by a just resentment against Denmark, and by his friendship for Frederick the Great. Policy, leagued with his moderation. For, the ruinous war which Elizabeth waged against the

the King of Pruffia, had coft her three hundred thoufand men, and above thirty millions of roubles.

Though the third Peter, had no other title to public efteem than that of faving a Prince, upon whofe prefervation the maintenance of the political equilibre depended, his memory fhould be regarded, and efteemed. In fome venal writings, the productions of fanciful hiftorians, his attachment to the King of Pruffia was ridiculed as the effect of enthufiafm, and

and the puerile love of emulation:—but assuredly an enthusiasm for, and admiration of, the qualities of a man, who wrought such prodigies of wisdom and intrepidity, was very excusable—and the heroism of friendship, is a rare quality amongst kings.

This profound respect, and regard, for Frederick the Great, demonstrated judgement and sensibility in the third Peter; the enemies of Prussia, at Petersburg, had signalized themselves, by the persecution of the young Czar, during

during the reign of Elizabeth.—
This Prince had accordingly counteracted their measures, and his subsequent conduct, in supporting the King of Prussia, was perfectly consistent.—This last monarch, was now in danger; the new English minister (Lord Bute) threatened him with desertion, and his safety seemed to depend on his Turkish negotiations, on the capricious motions, of the Khan of the Tartars.—Let us see in what terms, the hero so renowned for his knowledge of the human character, has appreciated the

the friendship, and generosity of the third Peter.

" The King had cultivated the
" friendship of the Great Duke,
" when he was only sovereign of
" Holstein; and by a grateful
" sensibility, rare amongst men,
" still more uncommon amongst
" princes, this Prince had pre-
" served a grateful heart, of
" which he had even given
" proofs, in the seven years war;
" for, it was he that principally
" contributed to the retreat of
" the Mareschal Apraxin, when
" he had worsted General Le-
wald,

"wald, and had retired towards
"Poland.—During these trou-
"bles, the Prince declined going
"to council, of which he was a
"member, that he might not
"participate in the measures,
"which he disapproved, against
"Prussia.—The King did not
"keep up the ordinary inter-
"course of politicians with this
"Prince, but acted with that
"cordiality which friendship re-
"quires, and which forms its
"most amiable appendage;—the
"virtues of Peter, were an ex-
"ception to the rules of politi-
"cians,

" cians, happy would it have
" been, if they had made an ex-
" ception for him."

Such was the teftimony, rendered to the memory of Peter the Third, twenty-five years after his cataftrophe, by the firft, and the moft penetrating genius, with the coolnefs of age, and the calm of reflection, in a pofthumous work dedicated to juftice, and to truth; the illuftrious author could not be fuppofed, to paint the character of the late Emperor of Ruffia, from the illufions of friendfhip; and,

were

were such a supposition possible, he would be contradicted by the well known authenticated, testimonies and histories of that unfortunate Monarch.

The first misfortune of this Prince was to be adopted by Elizabeth, to mount one day

Sur ce Throne glissant, dont vingt Rois descendirent—

The second, to have been led from Holstein, to become a slave at Elizabeth's court; and his wife was the third misfortune. His Imperial Aunt, obtained the crown by by a revolution stained with injustice, and was always in dread of a counter-revolution; her nephew was a prisoner of state. The cabinet was barred, and its councils were concealed; all intercourse was suspected with him; his German servants were deprived of the comforts of his conversation, and their attachment was a principle of disgrace; surrounded by enemies, the right of approach was only given to spies, observers, and betrayers of his conversation—his matrimonial misunderstanding left the Prince without domestic

domestic consolation, and reviewing some troops at Orienabaum, became his only recreation.

His complaints gave rise to an intrigue, which serves to lead us through the mazes of those deplorable events, which ultimately deprived the Emperor of his scepter, and of his life.

The Chancellor Bestuchef, the great confidant of Elizabeth, was the Grand Duke's avowed enemy; his insolence in contriving morti-

mortifications, made him tremble at the prospect of a new reign; he formed the project of substituting the Prince Paul, son of Catherine the Second, under her regency, in the place of Peter the Third. Bestuchef presupposed the success of his plot, from a multitude of groundless calumnies against the Grand Duke, and the favourable reception of Elizabeth; and lastly, upon the intention of Catherine to deprive her husband of the crown, and to appropriate the regency to herself. It would be presumptuous to advance,

vance, that this Princefs was concerned in this plot—but affuredly Beftuchef muft have believed it, for, he never would have encountered her refiftance. Elizabeth, doubtful at firft, refumed a more dignified conduct, and fupported her nephew againft the Chancellor; and an incautious expreffion of the Emprefs Elizabeth is ftill cited, " I know my nephew," faid fhe one day, to the flanderers of the Prince, " I have nothing to fear " from a good heart, I am not " fo well acquainted with my " niece."

Beftu-

Bestuchef, afterwards disgraced by Elizabeth, was excepted out of the amnesty, upon the accession of the third Peter; but upon the indulgence of Catherine, he was recalled from exile.

The preceding facts, which repose upon the authority of authentic historians, describe the first clouds of that tempest, in which the third Peter was involved; prudence could alone preserve him from the rocks, and breakers through which he passed;—but amongst his other virtues, he found one, namely, confidence, which caused his destruction.

Notwithstanding the reproaches justly cast upon that monarch, from the excess of his good qualities, spite of the blame with which he is attacked, upon the unfortunate career of his debaucheries, and of the slanders which hatred and remorse have attached to his memory, few princes have began to reign with more wisdom; his first public actions expiated the defects of many preceding years,

and

and they had only six months duration.

Siberia, and the state prisons, were filled with distinguished captives, victims of the favourites, and ministers of Elizabeth—the Emperor redressed their wrongs—the illustrious Munich was recalled, and reinstated—Biron, Lestock, and some of whom had offended him in the late reign, were restored to liberty; by a prince who extended his clemency to the insolent favourites of his Aunt—the first qualities of his government were justice and clemency—and his magnanimity to some Prussian officers, whom the fortune of war had deprived of liberty, and who groaned in extreme servitude, is too well known to be recorded.

The commencement of his reign promised zeal for promoting order, and discovered application, vigilance, and activity — he was early at the senate, at the different offices, and set an example of industry, by his superintendance in various departments: the first Peter was his model, and his plans formed the chart of his legisla-

legislation — to him Russia owes the wisest ordinances, which have decorated that government.

Not satisfied with limiting the despotism of his officers, he abridged his own power, by abolishing the secret council of chancery, a state inquisition, which, upon the least suspicion, imprisoned, tortured, or executed, natives, and strangers. He was a warm friend to toleration; and he framed that memorable decree, which enfranchised the nobles from compulsive service, and permitted them to travel, without the royal permission.

Precipitation, it is true, accompanied some of these salutary innovations; particularly those relating to the clergy. The secularization of Monks, was adopted from the design of Peter the Great. The Emperor secured to the regular clergy competent stipends, from their immence revenues; and with the surplus he founded schools, and military hospitals.—Reason and policy approved these measures, and the reforma-

reformation of superstitious worship; but these hasty changes shocked the customs and manners of the country; the strong hand of the first Peter could scarcely have effected their execution; but the Emperor accelerated these reforms, without reflecting, that they gave pretext to the designing, to render his government unpopular.

The regiments of Ismailoff and Preobrazinski, formed a body of guards, in barracks in Petersburg, licentious and ill disciplined, their want of subordination enervated their loyalty; and in former revolutions, they were fold to the highest purchaser. Peter the Third conceived, that a rigorous discipline would secure their obedience, and prevent the disorders of a body so badly organized, he introduced the Prussian discipline, modelled them after his Holstein guards, and secured order by severity: had this discipline been firmly established, their fidelity would have been secured; corruption is difficult in a corps inured to the daily detail of their duty;

duty; but the reformation was of neceffity entrufted to German, in preference to Ruffian, officers. Thefe ftrangers were confidered as ufurpers; their favour became the object of ridicule, and the national troops were inftigated to revolt, by the ignorant pride of being offended, at foreign inftruction.

When we reflect, that many of thefe wife regulations were in that fhort period of fix months, which put a period to the reign

of

of their author, we are affected by pity, and with horror.

Some of these innovations, deserved public gratitude, others, the reproach of precipitation—though a sovereign despot, this Prince excelled in acts of bounty, and of justice. His enterprises against Denmark, were more natural, and less pernicious, than the war against Prussia, fostered by the personal hatred of Elizabeth, and her minister. The private life of Peter, it is true, was disfigured by the excesses of the table,

table, which ultimately might have rendered him contemptible; but where is the king, or the individual, whose infirmities are not relieved by some good qualities?— Does not equity hold the balance, of good, and of bad qualities?— If the virtues and defects of the Emperor were weighed, who is there could justify his dethronement, and his death? Is the least equality visible, between the discontents he produced, and his unfortunate exit. A warm friend, a good father, an indulgent husband, but too easy, too confident, and

and too open to those traitors, upon whom his favours were lavished; at the end of six months, he experienced a fate, which ten years stained with crimes, and with tyranny, could have scarcely justified.

His unchangeable security, annihilates all those imputations which have burthened his memory; a conspiracy was secretly projected, of which he rejected the least suspicion—the loyal, trembled for his safety—clandestine assemblies directed by the partizans of the Empress, and their designs upon the Crown. The Prince George of Holstein, and other clear-sighted men, perceived his danger—confidential emissaries daily aggravated the conduct of Peter, poisoned the public discourse, and prepared the way for a revolution:—the Emperor alone remained fearless — solicited by discoveries, he rejected them as calumnies. Amongst those who wished to awaken him from his lethargy, was the King of Prussia. That wise, and penetrating monarch, has preserved an abridgement

ment of the letter, and the Emperor's answer; and both cast a great light upon the true cause of this revolution.

"The friendship of Frederick the Second, his esteem, as well as gratitude, his opinion of the excellent qualities of the third Peter, induced him to write, and to reveal these mysteries. He requested that his coronation might take place at Moscow, and that his person might thereby be rendered sacred, in the eyes of the nation.
"He

"He mentioned the revolutions, in Ruſſia, ſince the reign of Peter the Great; but touched them lightly, and finiſhed with conjuring that the Emperor would take proper precautions for his perſonal ſafety."

This letter made no impreſſion upon the Emperor—he anſwered it in theſe terms: "Touching the intereſt you expreſs for my ſafety, I requeſt you will reſt contented. I am called the father of my ſoldiers — they prefer a male to a female government:

"vernment: I walk alone constantly, in Petersburg—if any mischief is meditated, it would have been effected long since; but I am a general benefactor; I repose myself on the protection of Heaven, trusting to that; I have nothing to fear."

Notwithstanding this answer, the King of Prussia continued to inform Peter the Third of his danger. Messieurs Goltz and Schewrin has orders to converse with him on this subject, in their audiences; but it was to no purpose

pose that they told him, that while the customs of Russia prevailed, the Sovereign could not take too many precautions:—at last the king told them, "My friends, say no more upon that disagreeable subject."

Assuredly this was the language of candour, and it proves how averse the Emperor was to any of these bad designs, which were attributed to him, to colour the fatal conspiracy against his freedom, and his life. They knew but little of the human heart, and still less of an open character, which never disguised his thoughts, who do not find in the tranquillity of his conscience, the secret of his security.—Had Peter designed to imprison his wife, and his successor, her son, he could have watched all the motions of their partizans; he would have listened to the suspicions of his faithful servants, the admonitions of his friend, the Prussian monarch; the council he listened to, with such attention, would have produced explanation, and not that simple answer,

answer, "I am a general bene-
"factor, and therefore I have
"nothing to fear."

It is remarkable, that the first design, was to adopt the before-mentioned project of the Chancellor Bestuchef, which was to declare the young Duke to be Emperor, under the regency of his mother: this scheme was not a new plan of the Czarina's partizans; and the consideration of its forming the base of a new plot against the Emperor, shewed it had long been in contemplation, and was an artful

ful contrivance — they could not prevent his fucceffion; but they intended to dethrone him, by a continuation of the fame machinations.

This fyftem, however, had the objections of a minority; and if a regency would have been fhaken upon the firft popular difcontent, and upon his majority, the government of the Emprefs would terminate — and who could not anfwer that fhe might not experience the fate of her hufband. It was, therefore, refolved to dethrone

throne the father and the son, and to consummate their ambitious views, by placing this uncertain crown upon the head of the Empress.

Never was there a bolder project; but fortune favoured their audaciousness. Peter was on the wing for Holstein, and the conspirators chose the period of his absence, to possess the capital. Had this succeeded, Russia would have had two sovereigns, in Germany and in Petersburg, with all the convulsions attendant upon divided

divided sway. While the Czar lived, Catherine could not expect a tranquil moment—but it seems trivial circumstances accelerated the execution, aggravated the catastrophe, and secured success.

To his last day, even to his last hour, Peter preserved his magnanimous, fatal security, and confidence; his Russian guards were corrupted by Orlof, and Rozamouski; Catherine was mistress of the Capital, and his officers were seduced by slanders against their sovereign. Already had the conspi-

conspirators impiously counteracted their fidelity, by swearing and binding themselves in the most solemn manner, to commit high treason—and the Archbishop of Novogorod, that fanatic incendiary, whom the clemency of Peter had pardoned, presided in the solemnization of this ceremony, under the auspices of the Empress. At length the Emperor's friends were arrested, and the people were deceived by artful reports, that the Prince had died by a fall from his horse, before

fore Peter suspected the enterprize at Petersburg.

He was then at the Orienabaum. Spite of the baseness and servile infidelity of many nobles, of military and civil officers, he had still some resolute friends:—the Chancellor of Woronzof, the virtuous Mareschal Munich, and his faithful Holstein troops—affairs were not yet desperate—the intrepid Munich counciled Peter to march directly to Petersburg, at the head of his German troops:— " I shall precede you," said the generous

generous veteran, "and my dead body shall be a rampart to your sacred person." Possibly such a resolution would have crushed the conspirators;—the same servile spirit which had prostrated the nobles, the people, and the soldiery, would have reduced them to their lawful sovereign, marching to vindicate his crown with his sword, and with the abilities of Munich.

But alas! irresolution superseded courage; not that Peter wanted spirit, but he was distracted ed by discordant councils—in his train were emissaries of the Empress, bathing the hands of this Prince with deceitful tears, affecting to represent the dangers he incurred, and inviting him to the Empress, and deprecating resistance. This perfidy accomplished what treachery had commenced; and thus Peter, surrounded by traitors, was entangled in their snares, and a prey to uncertainty, when every moment was precious, and called for decision.

Europe

Europe, and posterity, will never forget the cruel fate of this monarch, in the flower of his age—dragged into captivity, and expiring in the ferocious hands of his wife, and his own confidents. The humane compassionated his misfortunes; and none that were insensible of his sufferings, save only those from whom he had a claim to succour, and to consolation.

On the contrary, outrages of every kind were offered to him: by delivering himself up voluntarily

tarily to her, who, during fourteen years, had the honour to be the partner of his bed, it seemed he was protected, by all that is moſt ſacred amongſt men. His perſon, committed to the diſcretion of the Empreſs, became a depoſit, upon which it was no longer permited to form attacks—it neither belonged to his enemies, by the rights of war, nor by that of the laws; and from the moment Peter had ſurrendered, without being compulſion, every abode of Catherine ſhould have been an inviolable aſylum for him:—alas! this

this illusion, by which he had been dazzled, was of a short duration.

He had been defamed by a manifesto of June the twenty-eighth;—hardly arrived at Peterhof, he became a prisoner, and felt the humiliation of being secretly visited by Count Panin, that frivolous and versatile minister, loaded with praises by hireling gazetteers—that Panin, who had dared to dictate to his master, and benefactor, to a sovereign, who was a prisoner, an act of abdication,

dication, and of dishonour; an act conceived in the most humiliating expressions—that Panin, at fine, who forced the descendant of Peter the First, to take his oath in the presence of the Almighty, and renounce his crown, to sign with his own hand such a monument of audaciousness, and infamy.

Notwithstanding this abdication, which served as a new title for preserving his life, and liberty, the Emperor, that very night, was confined in the castle of of Robfcha. Whilſt her huſband entered this tomb, the Empreſs ſurpriſed Peterſburg, with the noiſe and buſtle of a triumphal entry.

But this pageant was not ſufficient, to ſtifle the ſenſibility of the multitude; diſloyalty, in a vaſt number of them, was rapidly ſucceeded by remorſe, and by compaſſion. The people, who are always good, when left to their natural impulſe, were ſhocked at hearing that their ſovereign had juſt paſſed from a throne, into the

the horrors of an eternal prison. The soldiery manifested their emotions, every one was affected by the remembrance of Peter's virtues, and his faults were forgotten, as the displeasure hourly increased; the Empress was threatened with a frightful reverse.......
But let us draw a veil over this melancholy scene, which put an end to his inquietudes; let us not repeat, that the seventh day of his captivity, Peter the Third was no more; that he contended for his unhappy life, with the ferocious courtiers who penetrated into the

the fortress; that the screams of his convulsive agonies were heard; that two days after, some strangers saw the walls stained with the Emperor's blood; and that one of the principal performers in this tragedy, had been pursued for years, by the idea of his expiring sovereign, and exhibited a shocking spectacle in Petersburg; of remorse, and of insanity.

- At the first news of this catastrophe, Europe, though habituated to the bloody revolutions, which, for forty years, gave mas-

ters to Ruffia, fhewed lefs furprife, than compaffion: public opinion was favourable to the victim. In order to colour the facrifice, fictitious reports were circulated; finifter projects were imputed to Peter the Third, againft which, the Emprefs fhould have guarded herfelf;—" For," according to the remark of a celebrated writer, " nothing is fo
" eafy as to fuppofe crimes in
" thofe, who are already purfued,
" by the hatred of a victorious
" party.

This

This is not the time to anticipate the revelations of History; but there is no impropriety in presenting beforehand the justice of them, by observing how ridiculous those pretences were, with which the persecutors of Peter the Third, amused the credulity of the people.

In the manifesto of June the 28th, this Prince is accused *of having shaken the foundations of the Greek church, of the established religion; and of having given room to apprehend that another would be introduced*

introduced in its stead: the most frantic fanaticism could only have dictated such a charge. Peter had been tolerant; he authorised a Lutheran chapel at Orienabaum, for the use of his German troops; surly it cannot be pretended, that he should have compelled his soldiers, from Holstein, to follow, like himself, the rites and liturgy of the Greek church. His toleration was the consequence of the progress of reason, of the example of all the wise Princes of his time. When Joseph the Second had granted the Protestant congregations

gations in his dominions, the liberty of worſhip; none of his relations thought of contending with him for the Empire, under pretence that he ſhook the prevailing faith. This faith has no affinity with ſecularizing monaſteries, or diminiſhing the number of images, which the vulgar had worſhipped. Theſe reformations belong to religious diſcipline, and are not attempts againſt the dogmas of the eſtabliſhed religion. Is it for the intereſt of the god of peace and juſtice, to dethrone, to impriſon, to put to death, the legitimate

gitimate chief of the state? In fine, was it consistent for the tolerant Catherine, to render herself the interpreter, the avenger of some zealots' resentment, to sacrifice the duties of affinity, and of the throne to popular fanaticism?

The second grievance, alledged in the manifesto, is not less ludicrous. It is pretended that the glory of Russia has been, as it were, *trampled upon by the peace, lately concluded with its greatest enemy.* Neither the Russian government,

vernment, nor the nation, had the least reason to look upon the King of Prussia as their greatest enemy; the two powers had no grounds of dispute—Elizabeth's personal rancour, and the artifices of a perverse minister, who had been justly punished, had occasioned the war; there would have been glory in putting an end to it, rather than in persisting in spilling human blood, and wasting the treasures of the state, when her interests were not concerned; had not this truth been almost self-evident, Catherine herself would not

not have made it clear, by her subsequent conduct to this Prince, who had been rashly called the greatest enemy to *Russia*.

It is plain, then, that these reproaches are only evasions contrived by those, who are sorry for having no legitimate excuse. No sovereign could be, for four and twenty hours, sure of his crown, if it depended on accusations of that kind. It is true, that to these frivolous allegations, more serious ones were added by artful rumours, particularly of a plot formed

formed by the Emperor, against Catherine's liberty, and that of her son. But had this, and other similar designs existed, why were they not exposed in this accusatory manifesto? Why were not these legitimate complaints given, as a plea to justify such violent measures? Why has recourse been had to the danger of orthodoxy, to the peace with Prussia? Why have the dangers of religion, and the peace with Prussia been started, when it was possible to gain the good opinions of the people, by disclosing a conspiracy both

both against the partner of the throne, and his successor? If, at the moment of fixing the public opinion, these chimerical attempts had been unnoticed, is it not probable, that they were contrived afterwards, in order to silence the clamours of the public?

Besides, many notorious facts destroy these assertions, of which no admissible proof has ever been produced. It is known, that at the time of setting out for Holstein, Peter had named the Empress regent during his absence.

Who can believe, that he thus trusted the government of his capital, the administration of his empire, to a Princess whom he intended to arrest? It would be an idle task to expatiate upon these irreconcileable ideas.

But in the fortress of Schluffelbourg, Peter, as was reported, had an apartment constructed seemingly for an illustrious person, who was reported to be the Empress. The fact is certain, that an apartment was constructed, but the inference is erroneous.
There

There is an anecdote which unravels this mysterious incident; the learned and accurate Busching, upon his return from Russia, had published this secret; he had been apprized of it by General Korff, who had accompanied Peter III. to Schluffelbourg; particular informations have confirmed the truth, and discovered some circumstances of this story, which we shall here transcribe.

In March, 1762, Peter III., accompanied by General Korff, and Mr. Goudewitz, repaired, incognito,

cognito, to Schluffelbourg, where Elizabeth, in 1756, had caused the unfortunate Prince Iwan to be transferred, who had a right to the throne, by the Empress Ann, Duchess of Courland, his Aunt.

He was proclaimed Emperor in 1740, when in his cradle; he was deposed by Elizabeth in 1741; he was imprisoned and assassinated in 1764. Peter was affected at seeing the manner in which this prisoner was treated: an arched room, twenty feet square,

square, formed his habitation; a truckle bed, with a table and a few chairs, were all his furniture; hardly a faint light pervaded this sorrowful dwelling; by degrees, the Prince was weaned of most of the comforts bestowed upon him, before the former years of his captivity. In his conversation with the Emperor, he inveighed against the Grand Duke and his consort, styling them the usurpers of his crown. " I shall re- " gain it," added he, " and will " have them both beheaded." Peter, less affected by this discourse,

course, than the deplorable condition of the Prince, whose senses were affected, and bore in every respect a stamp of imbecility, assured him that the Grand Duke did not bear him any ill will, and would be much concerned at his situation, if he were apprized of it.—" I approach his
" person very often," added he,
" and if you wish for an allevia-
" tion of your imprisonment, I
" promise to obtain it for you."
The Prince answered, with a sigh, that " one day he had been
" permitted to come down into
" the

"the inner court of the fortress, he had looked at the sky, and breathed a pure air; it is," added he, "the most ravishing pleasure I have ever enjoyed; and if the Grand Duke be not an enemy to me, tell him, I pray you, that I beg he would grant it to me very often." Peter could not help melting into tears, and from that moment resolved to set Iwan at liberty: such was likewise the sentiment of Prince George of Holstein, the Emperor's uncle; but the insanity of the prisoner having been proved,

proved, Peter determind to have a convenient house built in the fortress for him, with a terrace, that he might take a walk every day. Whilst that building was constructing, Iwan was transferred to Kexholm, at the other extremity of the lake Ladoga. Three weeks after, the Emperor was dethroned; and as if this were a consequence of the fear with which the new building, at Schluffelbourg, had inspired his enemies, he perished a victim of his humane and generous sentiments.

Iwan survived him only two years: a new mysterious tragedy put an end, on the 5th of July, 1764, to the alarms which this Prince, though fettered, had created. It is well known that he had been assassinated by his own guards; and that after such a crime, the only blood spilt upon a scaffold at Petersburg, was that of Lieutenant-general Mirovitch, who had been arraigned for attempting to defend the life of a grand nephew to Peter the Great.

Such

Such were the auspices under which the new Empress began to reign—the circumstances of her elevation determined her eagerness for glory. She was conscious she should keep the Russians constantly employed, fix their attention upon enterprizes and conquests, and foreign sway; to strengthen her power at home.

It has been mentioned, that the deposition of Peter, and the Empress's manifesto, were solely founded upon his plans and connections with Prussia; but these, truly patriotic plans, though previously condemned by her, have all been executed by Catherine II.; and it is to them this Princess is indebted for the most solid part of her glory. On the other side, upon the Emperor's ashes, was laid the foundation of a close connection with the King of Prussia, who before had been declared the natural enemy of Russia.

Uncertain of the measures Frederick the Great would take, being afraid lest he should employ against herself the corps that,

under

under Mr. de Czernichef, had joined the Prussians, she hastily recalled her troops; but they remained inactive; and as soon as the Empress had secured her authority, she adopted Peter the Third's policy, soothed Prussia, and soon attached herself to her, by a defensive alliance.

Peter had done so through principle; Catherine did it in order to prepare enterprizes conformable to her genius and situation, to the ambition of the minions who surrounded her person: having formed the plan of imposing her laws upon her neighbours, it was important for her to keep fair with the power that could assist them. Denmark was almost gained over, Sweden was governed by a faction corrupted by Russia; Poland was deprived of the most solemn act of sovereignty, that of electing a king; in fine, Courland did no longer exist, but to be a prey to the caprice of the councils of Petersburg.

CHAP.

CHAP. III.

The Usurpation of the Duchy of Courland.

THE Duchy of Courland and Semi-gallia, abounding in corn, rich from its naval stores, containing fifteen hundred thousand inhabitants, governed by a warlike nobility, possessing on the Baltic two advantageous ports, forms, by its situation, an important barrier between the new dominions

dominions of the Russian empire, Prussia, and Poland. Since the Swedes have lost Livonia, Courland, in time of war, becomes necessary to supply them with provisions. In that respect, the neighbourhood of Petersburg must be very dangerous to Courland, which is thereby rendered exceedingly useful to Russia, in cases of necessity. It has been, for these fifty years, treated like a Moscovite province; but the affronts have been multiplied, and the yoke made heavier under the reign of Catherine II.

When

When she seized upon the reigns of government, the Prince Charles of Saxony, the second son of Auguſt III., poſſeſſed Courland. He had in his favour the free choice of the ſtates, the free homage of the nobility, the ſolemn inveſtiture of the king, and the republic of Poland, of which Courland is a fief. Having been inſtalled in 1759, and acknowledged by all the powers, he united every right of lawful poſſeſſion.

This poffeffion did not prevent the Emprefs of Ruffia, in 1762, affixing her feal upon the property of the domain of Courland, and exercifing a pofitive act of fovereignty. She wanted a Duke of her own creation, and devoted to her interefts—to whom did fhe give the preference?—to that Erneft John Biren, declared guilty of high treafon by Elizabeth, banifhed to Siberia, dead in law, and fo fentenced by a decree of the ftates of Courland. Though recalled, it is true, fince, Elizabeth's death, his degradation did

no

no longer permit her to promote him again to an elective sovereignty, which, even in its origin, had never been lawful; for, Biren had evaded the personal homage he owed the republic of Poland, and the neglect of which made his investiture void.

If, however, Biren's pretensions were less warrantable, there existed only one competent judge of it, the Sovereign. It belonged to Poland to decide upon her vassal's reclamation; August the Third was so moderate as to refer this exami-

examination to the Empress's decision.

Instead of using negotiations, the Empress forced the inclination of the inhabitants of Courland from the arbitration of their legitimate sovereign from Poland, the Lord Paramount of this fief. At first emissaries attempted to corrupt the loyalty of the nobles, and to stir them up against the Duke Charles. The expedients having failed, strange outrages were tried —the Duke lived at Mittau; he was expelled from that place.—
The

The most attrocious indignities, preceded such a violation of the right of nations, of the right of sovereigns, of respect, and decency. M. de Simolin, a native of Courland, and then minister of the Russian cabinet, and of its tyranny, at Mittau, formed the plan of famishing the Prince Charles, and he put it into execution; he began with seizing and sequestering the revenues of the demesnes; aftewards, the archives were carried away; at length, Russian guards closed the magazines of wood, of straw, and of oats,

oats, the brewhouse, cellars, storehouses, fountains, and even the poultry yard of his Royal Highness. This execution of a new kind was followed by acts equally outrageous:—Biren was then introduced into Mittau, and installed by M. de Simolin's soldiers. That agent of the Czarina treated the magistrates of Mittau, the States, the King of Poland's deputies, like his servants:— but the Prince Charles persisted to remain in Courland; Count Brown, Governor of Livonia, sent him orders that he should *leave the country*,

for,

for, such was the Empress's pleasure. This haughty command was effected, in spite of the lawful sovereign still resisting to the last; and thus was treated, in his own dominions, in the presence of an independent nation, a Prince, the son and vassal to the King of Poland, an ally of Russia.

Of that former encroachment upon the liberties of Courland, and the rights of Poland, the compleat reduction of the Duchy was the consequence. Ten thousand Russians, after forcing them

them to receive a king, elected at Peterſburg, compelled them to ſecure Erneſt John Biren's ſon, the inveſtiture of Courland: Peter, the new Duke, was permitted to preſerve his dignity, but on condition that he ſhould ſubmit to the orders, and yield to the Extorſions of the Empreſs's minions:—the firſt employments of Courland were conferred upon their creatures, and claims were ſilenced; thoſe were diſmiſſed, who could not be ſeduced; thoſe were ſeduced, who, through an apparent good character,

-ter, were likely to form an opposition. Among the latter, was the Chamberlain Howen, distinguished for his capacity and courage; having defended, at Warsaw, the rights of his native country against the Russian despotism, he was seized, carried off, and sent to Siberia; and he was under the necessity of choosing either the sacrifice of his patriotism, or that of his liberty: but he stooped to wear the common chain, governed Courland in the name of the Empress, and was promoted to the dignity of Bourgrave. Marshal Klopman,

Klopman, his predecessor in authority, had adopted the same condescension. Under the influence of those tools of the Empress, the Duke's authority has been, in fact, annihilated — the suffrages of the states have been bought publicly — vexations of every kind, alienations, political robberies, have been legalized. At the voice of the Russian minister at Mittau, Courland narrowed her limits, suffered her own subjects, reclaimed as Russians, to be carried away, subjected her policy to the rescripts of the Empress's

Empress's councils. More than once, the Duke, reduced to the title of his principality, saw himself forced to buy its preservation. Every murmur he risked, was answered by a menace; *and the menace was* immediately followed by an extortion. At last, fatigued with so expensive a tutelage, he sought for protectors less exacting—The Empress had treated him like a rebel. Prudence had suggested to him an escape; he took refuge at Berlin; secured part of his treasure there, and meditated a plan of abdication.

At the first indication of such a design, which was in favour of one of the Princes of Virtemberg, engaged in the service of Prussia, as it was imagined, the Empress addressed a strong admonition to the States of Courland, and threatened them with her indignation, if they presumed to concur in this opinion. Thus, after having despoiled the reigning Duke of his authority, she insisted he should keep the shadow of it—she forbade Courland to use her sovereign right of choosing a successor to the Duchy. Thus Russia declared to to all Europe, that she had no respect, no regard, due by sovereigns to their mutual independence; that for her sake, all those rights should be effaced which are the basis of society; that she laid an undeniable claim to the dictatorship over such states as were placed by Providence in her neighbourhood.

Courland, insensible from fear or corruption, had suffered this outrage — the Duke returned to Mittau — the crisis was favourable to men, roused by a just sense of public injury—the court of Berlin still perceives the effect of Ruffian influence in Courland, which extends to the frontiers of Poland. The true intereſt of this country would have aided her defigns, if fhe had power to aid her with fuccefs.

CHAP.

CHAP. IV.

Affairs of Poland—Nomination of Staniſlaus the Third by Ruſſia.

THE Empreſs had hardly dethroned one ſovereign, before ſhe undertook to create another in Poland. At the death of Auguſtus the Third, probably the court of Peterſburg did not comprehend all the ſchemes at firſt view which were neceſſary to carry this plan into execution, but

but which were produced and disclosed by degrees. The present policy proceeded no farther than to reduce Sweden to inactivity, and thereby to exercise a decisive influence, to form and to excite factions one against the other, and to facilitate that work of Count Panin, the northern league, which might certainly have insured to Russia a supremacy over all the adjoining countries.

The concurrence of Prussia was necessary for the completion of this plan; it was the interest of of that king to detach Ruffia from Vienna—he was averfe to the Houfe of Saxony, and to their pretenfions to Poland. Since the peace, he had fkilfully engaged the Emprefs and Count Panin in his interefts, and had negotiated a treaty at Peterfburg. Catherine, determined to have the afcendant in Poland, formed an alliance with Pruffia, to counterbalance the Saxon, Auftrian, and French oppofition. In January, 1764, the two courts figned a defenfive alliance. Frederick himfelf informs us, that they

they engaged to prevent the Crown becoming hereditary in Poland; to name a Piaſt or Protector, namely, Staniſlaus Poniatouſki, Stolnick or governor of Lithuania, to protect the Diffidents, or in juſter terms, to arm them againſt the Commonwealth.

The court of Peterſburg was the party principally intereſted in this plan, to whom the advantage would belong—Pruſſia had only a collateral intereſt, namely, that of favouring the deſign of her ally.

The

The force and energy of the best historian cannot describe the execution and the horrible consequences of this enterprize; they are the disgrace of this century—the most unprincipled politician could hardly premeditate a system of violence and oppression similar to that under which Poland has groaned for ten successive years.

Waving the criminations of partizans, events of public notoriety afford the most ample testimony.

To exclude all foreign candidates from an elective sovereignty, was a glaring violation of the constitution of an independant country, which could alone claim the disposition of its crown; but the sole fiat of Russia superseded every other consideration; and a foreign Prince, who might have force or ability to defend the republic, could not be convenient for the designs of Russia.

A sovereign who should be her nominee, and not the choice of his countrymen, was necessary—
A Rad-

A Radzivil, a Potocki—any noble possessed of reputation, of independance, would not have become a royal pageant, dependant upon a foreign Prince.

The King which she wanted, was one of a mild and flexible character; insulated, unconnected, without any relation or alliance with any other power in Europe—the legality of whose election should render him obnoxious to the people, to a host of enemies, and consequently forced

forced to rely upon that power and protection to which he had owed his elevation.

All thefe qualifications appeared in the character of Staniflaus the Third—a good difpofition, improved by education, thofe amiable qualities which ingratiate individuals, and gain general regard and efteem. His poverty, his youth, his connections with Ruffia, the marked favour of the Emprefs, would have prevented his fucceffion to this painful pre-eminence. This election could never

never be due to free suffrages; but to a violation of national privileges. This prince, it is presumed, hoped to regain public affection by time; but Russian policy created a lasting alienation.

Upon the convention of the Diet, ten thousand Russians entered Warsaw, while the Prussians menaced the frontiers of the Republic. The districts which chose members, were filled by soldiers, who compelled the nomination of Russian partizans— the capital was soon surrounded by by Cossacks, who invested the Diet—their chamber was attacked — one of their members was arrested, and attacked, sword in hand, in this sanctuary of sovereign power, in the presence of the President or Marechale of the Diet, who left the assembly with the emblem of his office, accompanied by many illustrious senators, and other patriotic members, protesting against these violations of the laws of nations, and the liberty of Poland. Retiring into the provinces, they were followed by the Russians, who seized some who

who resisted, proscribed others, and declared Prince Radzivil an enemy to his country—these despotic proceedings were followed by breaches and innovations in the constitution. The four regiments of guards, under the King's authority, united with the Russian troops to interrupt the freedom of election—this tumultuous assembly, influenced by fear, elected and crowned Staniflaus. Exile or submission was the lot of his opponents, while Russia meditated new outrages.

It cannot be denied, that in many antecedent interregnums, recommendations, power, the violence of party, had favoured one or the other of the candidates; but a military force, and foreign troops, had never, before this, created a king in a free country, in the midst of his equals—of the lawful electors—of a nation thus influenced in her choice; nor could Voltaire, or other flatterers, justify this proceeding by precedent. —all former elections had been as peaceable as could be supposed, where numerous, independent, and

and sanguine partizans were convened—transitory tumults are not civil wars. Thus Henry of Valois, Ladislas the Fourth, Casimir, and Sobieski, had been elected. In divisions, or in double returns, or contested elections, as in the cases of Stephen Battori, Sigismond the Third, the Emperor Maximilian, a Polonese party had given the law—public liberty was not undermined, and troops never entered the district of election; no competitor had forced a nomination by his armies, though they might have afterwards supported

ported his election. Charles the Twelfth had, it is true, dethroned a King of Poland by war; but Auguſtus had provoked the indignation of the Alexander of the North. The active partizan of the Czar loſt his crown by the fortune of that war, in which his imprudence had engaged the republic.

Ruſſia was the firſt to give the example of a forced, and of a warlike military election: ſhe did not confine herſelf to countenance a free choice, but ſhe influenced

fluenced the preliminary steps, and prefaced her proceedings by forcing those places, which chose members, to return her partizans—these preparatory scenes were viewed in their true light by many foreign ministers, representatives of ancient allies, who retired from a country they could no longer consider as free under a military protectorate.

Sectaries and Dissenters, a numerous body, were excluded, under the Saxon Kings, from places of trust and employments in the state;

state; but the tolerating spirit of the republic, the mildest perhaps in Europe, gave them more freedom than in any other country; even in those where philosophy is most predominant. When Russia had excited their discontent, they had two hundred churches, beside places of private worship; they possessed governments, regiments, and military rank; most of the subalterns were non-conformists; their toleration was greater than that of the Dissenters in England, in Holland, in France, and even Russia herself. Political

cal dignities, it is true, were reserved to the established religion; but every other description of civil liberty was theirs—the republic was ever ready to redress their particular and accidental grievances

Of grievances, of which few had complained, Russia formed the materials of discontent. The Starofte, and the General Graboufki, two brothers, who were Diffenters, were bribed, and prevailed upon to display their grievances: they claimed the rights of

the

the treaties of Velau and Oliva, where Ruſſia was not concerned as a contracting, or an acceding, party; but ſhe arrogated the right of a guarantee; while Sweden, to whom this right really belonged, was ſilent. The treaty of Moſcow was falſely quoted, no ſtipulations having been created thereby in favour of the Diſſenters. At laſt the Diet, in 1766, heard their complaints, and redreſſed them, and reſtored ſuch rights as juſtice, law, and reaſonable toleration, allowed; but rejected ſuch as the common order eſtabliſhed

blished in all countries had forbidden; the legal barriers were left between the established religion and the tolerated sects, and excluded the sectaries from all political dignities.

Few states are governed by other regulations; of all other Princes, the Empress was the least qualified to demand their repeal: in her states Dissenters never entered into her councils, or administration, or had ever mounted the throne. Had the third Peter effected such an innovation,

vation, the apologists of the Empress, the writers of her manifestos, would have proclaimed the danger of the church, and of orthodoxy, as they did that of the pecuniary interests of the Monks.—This philosophical toleration, for which they inflamed Poland, did not prevent the schismatic Greeks, under Russian influence, to massacre a hundred thousand men, of a different persuasion, for which no Russian officer was questioned. Many Greeks and Latins, who were pillaged of their all, were seen in the Polish provinces, without

out the least effort of Russia to redress their grievances.

These remarks would hardly have taken place, had it not been for the number of violences in Poland, under the colour of toleration; but the plan was formed to oppress the republic, to protect a faction, and to maintain a standing Russian army. The policy of the court extended its baneful influence still farther; the equal rights of the Dissenters once established, a Dissenter might occupy the throne, under the auspices

spices of Ruffia and of her troops, which could level all difficulties. The Greek religion was interested in the designs against the republic, and their influence, in the eastern and southern provinces secured.

The moderate resolutions of the Diet, in 1766, were considered as acts of rebellion at Petersburg—From that moment the Prince Repnin, the ambassador at Warsaw, became Viceroy of the republic; the Dissenters were

were armed, and invoked public protection, while, united with the Ruffian troops, they betrayed the country.

But the defign of defending them openly, with the undecided declarations of the King of Pruffia, were not fufficient for the rapid execution of their defigns. The King of Poland murmured at the rigorous tutelage of himfelf, his family, and his party. To give fome energy to the national affemblies, they had abolifhed lished the Liberum Veto*, and some other wise regulations, which gave umbrage to Russia.

In consequence of this, the Russian dictator, under the modest name of an Ambassador, opposed artfully to the King, the nominee of the Empress, the members who had been exiled for their opposition to his election. Various

---

* A curious account of this power, which resembled the tribunitial power in the Roman State, is to be found in Mr. Coxe's Northern Tour.

intrigues

intrigues suceeded in 1765; and in 1767, conciliations were proposed; and it was with the olive branch in his hand, Prince Repnin prepared a poison for the Commonwealth.

By artful intrigues among the most discontented of the citizens, the Russian Ambassador formed the association at Radom, where the malecontents assembled in 1767, when the Catholicks and some nobles were gained by promises of satisfying their grievances; and it is an authenticated fact, that

that he proceeded so far as to assure some of them, that the King should be dethroned.

The Prince Radzivil, who had been exiled as the most active opponent of Russia, became the pillar of this new confederacy; he was named President of the association; but, under pretence of an escort, he became, in fact, a prisoner of State.

The Confederacy itself, surrounded by Russian troops, experienced the same fate:—at this period, he enjoined the convention of a Diet at Warsaw, for the redress of their grievances; and mixing derision with violence, he procured an embassy to the Empress, to thank her for her maternal care. The Confederates perceived in vain the nets in which they were entangled.

This memorable Diet opened in 1767;—the Russian troops had dictated the choice of many of their members;—the Grand Cup Bearer of the Crown had been imprisoned at Pologna, and the republic

republic appeared like a conquered ſtate. One of the members, who had courage to exclaim againſt their proceedings, was ſeized in the ſtreet; the Poles, ſo formidable hitherto to Ruſſia, were beſieged by their ſoldiery in their own ſenate houſe, and the legiſlators were invited to ſanction the orders of a Ruſſian plenipotentiary.

Among theſe decrees of Prince Repnin, one was, to admit the Schiſmatick Greeks and Diſſenters into political dignities, which would

would annihilate the independence of Poland, and convert it into a Ruffian province.

Soltyk, Bifhop of Cracovie, a man worthy of ancient Rome, having animated the courage of the Diet, and fpoken loudly againft thefe proceedings, was feized in his bed; while the Bifhop of Kiovie, and the Count of Cracovie, Rewufki, and his fon, underwent the fame fate, and were banifhed to Siberia. Warfaw was treated like a city taken by affault —thus were all Prince Repnin's decrees

decrees paſt, and thus did he pacify the Republic.

"So many acts of ſovereignty," ſays the King of Pruſſia, "exerciſed in the dominions of the Republic, by a foreign power, at length affected the public mind;" ſome Poles, whom deſpair had aſſembled in the Ukrain, gave the ſignal; the confederation of Bar was formed, which daily increaſed, and oppoſed the tyranny of Ruſſia. Unhappily this increaſing reſiſtance was but faintly, if at all, ſupported by any foreign

foreign court, which enabled the Russians to complete their work. For some time successes were balanced; but the Confederates being left to themselves, and fickle and unsteady in their plans and operations, were of no other use than to increase the barbarity of the Russian generals. One of them, Colonel Drewitz, ordered his prisoners' hands to be cut off, before they were executed. Monasteries, churches, neither age nor sex, were spared; no asylum was inviolate; the estates and properties of the Confederates, and of many others in Poland, were plundered, without distinction of ranks, or the rules of war in civilized countries; many prisoners of rank were exiled, and perished for want in the deserts of Siberia.

In the midst of these horrors, the Ottoman Port had declared she would resist encroachments upon her territory, and assist an old and useful ally, and prevent the torrent which inundated Poland from overflowing her possessions.

CHAP.

CHAP. V.

The Influence of the Russian Court in Denmark.

THIS rupture occupied not only Russia, but the courts of Berlin and Vienna. The Empress had condemned the northern courts to inactivity; in the name of the senate, she governed Sweden; Denmark was influenced by her Ambassadors.

She had reason to fear that the latter would avail herself of this crisis, to form alliances to support her ancient, undecided claim to the Duchy of Sleswick. Frederick the Fifth was still living. The Empress sent her privy counsellor Saldern to the Danish court, whose manners and whose haughtiness were analogous to the character of his country.

He displayed at Copenhagen the same haughtiness which even the King of Prussia had complained ed of at Berlin. The King of Denmark foon found that a Ruffian influence prevailed in the choice of his minifters and generals, and he concluded his miffion by the propofition of an amicable arrangement of an exchange for the Duchy of Slefwick.

Frederick the Fifth died before this treaty was concluded: Saldern afterwards appeared as a tutor to the new king; he prevailed upon him to travel, againft the opinion of his minifters, and the wifhes of the nation. Saldern, and

and Philosophoff, his subsequent colleague, became the arbiters and directors of the councils of Denmark; of the schemes, the political, and even private, affairs of the Danish monarch. Their dictatorship was absolute and uncontroled, and consequently highly unpopular. In 1767, they prevailed with the king to sign the provisional treaty for the Duchy of Slefwick, and their power might have been as durable as it was considerable, had it not been suddenly limited by that revolution which put a period to the

the administration of Rantzaw and Struenfee.

Seeing Ruffia weakened by the Turkish war, obliged to keep thirty thousand men in pay to guard Poland; her finances exhausted, and apprehensive of internal commotions; Struenfee attempted to conciliate Denmark with Sweden, the affairs of which latter he would no longer embroil: and to found in the North a political balance against the ambition of Ruffia; but the destiny of this country got the better. The unfortuate fortunate Struenfee's fchemes perifhed along with him, and Denmark felt the yoke once more; fhe joined again the train of Ruffia, and made a compact which forced her to interfere in all the difputes of that power, that is to fay, to defend her whenever her attempts upon the liberty of the North fhould be refifted. From Poland, from the Porte, the Emprefs had nothing to dread, but negotiations, or rather intrigues; and no real affiftance of a power of the firft order, or of the court of Vienna. This laft court did not

not look with an indifferent eye upon the afcendancy of Ruffia. The rapid progrefs of her fchemes, and of her arms, alarmed the Divan, and with much more reafon than the neighbouring powers. The Houfe of Auftria felt the danger of feeing near her frontiers a power accuftomed to refpect no boundaries. The Ottoman Porte being once crufhed, Poland fubdued, and the Danube poffeffed by the Ruffians, this ftorm muft needs envelope Hungary and the bordering provinces. Even the King of Pruffia, though an ally to Ruffia, was apprehenfive left, in procefs of time, fhe would attempt to give her laws to himfelf, as well as to Poland: at this period of common danger, he conciliated the court of Vienna: a fact worthy of the greateft attention, the certainty of which is eftablifhed by Frederick the Second himfelf, and from which, in this prefent juncture, the North, and all Germany, may derive much light. The greateft genius which ever fat upon a throne, and one of the moft penetrating ftatefmen, (Prince Kaunitz)

nitz) saw the neceffity of putting an end to the ambitious schemes of Ruffia, which, however, she resumed, and had almost accomplished without interruption.

CHAP.

CHAP. VI.

The Partition of Poland.

THE dismemberment of Poland was the result of this conflict, of interests and negotiations. All the blame must fall upon that power, whose ambition, kindling that of her neighbours, forced them, upon pain of a general war, to subscribe to that injustice, the disgrace of our age—To subscribe, we say, for not only the pretensions and violences of the Court of Petersburg, did no longer allow proper means for their termination; but the Empress herself was the first who justified this scandalous partition.—In that respect, opinion has long varied; but Frederick the Second has thrown a ray of light upon it, in that immortal work, which may be considered as his last testament, wherein he has deposited a recital of his faults with so much candour, and of his exploits with so much modesty.

L " The

"The Empress of Russia," says this great man, "being irritated that any other troops than her own should give law to Poland*, said to the Prince Henry, that if the Court of Vienna intended to dismember Poland, other neighbouring powers had a right to do the same. . . . . Count Solms, the Prussian Envoy, was charged to discover whether there was any solid meaning in these

---

* The King of Prussia here alludes to the sequestration of the county of Zips by some Austrian troops.

"expres-

" expreffions which the Emprefs
" had dropped; or if they had
" been uttered in a moment of
" humour and tranfitory paffion.
" Count Panin was rather averfe
" to that difmemberment, but the
" Emprefs entertained the flatter-
" ing idea of extending, without
" danger, the limits of her domi-
" nions. Her minions and fome
" of her minifters fupported her
" opinions. This refolution was
" prefented to the King of Pruf-
" fia, as an expedient contrived
" to indemnify him for the fub-
" fidies he had paid to Ruffia."

This Leonine convention met, however, with great difficulties from the Ruffians; they would not part either with Moldavia or Valachia, which they had poffeffed—the court of Vienna never would have affented to that ufurpation.—The King of Pruffia rifqued all the danger, the Emprefs had all the advantages, of this partition. The Czarina's minifters wore out the time in fubtlety and procraftination, in order to abforb the whole profit of this enterprize: at length the firmnefs of two of the contracting courts checked

checked her inflexible rapacity, and in February, 1772, the treaty was concluded, in a lefs iniquitous proportion of joint injuftice.

We fhall not dwell upon this fcandalous period of our hiftory, or the infringement of focial rights — the contempt of all remonftrances — the dreadful menaces — the outrages of every kind — by the help of which, the ratification of this ufurpation was extorted from the Diet of Poland. — The Ruffian Ambaffador acted the principal part in that fcene;

he

he alone conducted the plan. The degree of arrogance in those diplomatic oppressors may be easily conceived, after, by a letter from Mr. Saldern, to Count Oginski, Grand-General of Lithuania, the 21st of June, 1771, the Russian Envoy wrote to this magnat, one of the first personages in Poland, " The Ambassador repeats to you " the orders of his sovereign, " that you should repair to War- " saw, if ever you should wish " to deserve her protection: " should you neglect this intima- " tion, you will feel the conse- " quence:

" quence:—I need not have re-
" courſe to threats."

During theſe unprecedented violences, ſome Ruſſian Emiſſaries, and ſome hireling gazetteers, complimental apologiſts, and venal writers, flatterers who were reciprocally flattered, repreſented the Poles as a troop of fanaticks, and a gang of rebels. The Empreſs's manifeſtos themſelves were replete with ſuch epithets—In one of her letters to Voltaire, ſhe calls thoſe confederates whom her generals had plundered, maſſacred,

sacred, or exiled to Siberia, the mutineers of Poland. Voltaire, delighted with these philosophical conquests, invented a new language of adulation; he styled Catherine the Second, the northern star, and he became the high priest of her temple; a hundred pensioned authors repeated this fulsome adulation in Germany, and at Paris.

The republic, whose frontiers were destroyed, her demesnes lost, the citizens slain or proscribed, had no other expectation left,

left, but to see a seal put to the annihilation of her independence. She was compelled to refer the examination of her conqueror's projects to a delegation, where a venal and corrupt man presided, whose peculation had been discovered by the Diet, when she had recovered her liberty. Two distinct acts were carried by the contracting powers; the first, to sanction the dismemberment; the second, to fix the form of her government. Notwithstanding her melancholy situation, and the peremptory orders sent to the Diet,

only

only fifty-five Nuncios, against fifty-four, assented to the partition; nearly one half of the representatives of the equestrian order were absent or removed. As for the plan of a new constitution, it adopted all the defects of the old government of Poland, introduced pernicious novelties, and deprived the legislature of the power of correcting its own laws. By the most destructive of these new institutions, the interpretation of the laws, and almost the whole exercise of the executive power, were united in a permanent

manent council, whose superintendance lasted near two years. This council, thus constituted, constantly assembled, necessarily predominated over the general council, which met only six weeks in a twelvemonth.

Such an organization of the government necessarily facilitated foreign influence; for it was much easier to corrupt a body which consisted of few members, than such an assembly as the Diet. Russia deemed this species of constitution to be subservient to her design designs and interests, and she proposed and supported it with her whole strength; while the republick, for different reasons, gave it a strenuous opposition.

The king himself, supported by a majority of the Diet, rejected these insidious decrees, which were artfully called reformations. A whole year of intrigues, of bribery, and of threats and menaces, was necessary to surmount these difficulties, and to overcome this last resistance.

These

These measures were revived in the following year, and took place in 1776. When they were proposed to the Diet, in order to complete and ratify this revolution, in the beginning of that year, Stanislaus Potocki, the Nuncio, or representative of Lublin, speaking before this regenerated assembly, which professed an intention to restore Poland to her rank amongst the powers of Europe, thus described that Diet in 1776: " This Diet," said he, " violated the most sacred na-
" tional rights; every free and
" indepen-

" independent Pole faw himfelf
" expelled from that place, which
" fhould have been regarded as
" the fanctuary of liberty — the
" fenate houfe was furrounded
" by foldiers, and accefs was
" denied to every virtuous, pa-
" triotic, and public-fpirited
" member of the Diet."

The act of the 15th of March, 1775, which conftituted the permanent Council, and all the new laws, (it fhould be remembered) were figned only by the Ruffian minifter: the Envoys of the two other

other contracting powers have never ratified these institutions, although their concurrence and signature were necessary; and the republic gave positive instructions to that effect to the delegation which was empowered to treat with them; but Russia considered this as a meer matter of form, and passed by this neglect and fundamental nullity in their proceedings.

She not only compelled Poland to accede to this treaty, so ruinous to herself, and so advantageous to to Russia, but she imposed the yoke of her own perpetual guarranty upon all the new laws, whether they had a reference to police, revenue, or constitutional arrangement, which was proclaimed with drums and trumpets at the gates of Warsaw. This was the last mortal stroke to this expiring commonwealth;—from henceforward, the name of Poland was erased from the catalogue of nations; she was no longer, it is true, plundered by her protectors, or invaded by her auxiliaries; but the Russian Ambassador

bassador became the Viceroy of Poland, his creatures were the exclusive members of the Permanent Council, his troops garrisoned her fortresses, and a series of servile Diets introduced that lethargy which generally accompanies the loss of liberty.

Europe, from this period, considered Poland as a vassal of the Empress, until the day of retribution arrived;—a secret discontent announced its approach—the disposition of the country, and the Turkish war, accelerated her eman-

emancipation. The Republic saw with indignation, her southern provinces swarming with Russian troops, burthened by their magazines, infested by their foraging and recruiting parties, treated as tributaries, and subjected to all the horrors of the war between Russia and Turkey. When the Diet was assembled, a powerful sovereign * addressed a celebrated memorial to them, which gave light and information to their

---

* Frederick William, the present King of Prussia.

councils, and stimulated the energy of their proceedings. The result of his generous efforts and laudable exertions will form a brilliant page in the annals of the eighteenth century.

CHAP. VII.

Turkish Wars—Oriental System of Russia.

THE events which we have related, are only the first links of that chain with which Russia had designed to bind Europe; but her system extended farther. The fidelity of the Ottoman Porte to fulfil her engagements with Poland, broached designs which were meditated in the time of Peter

Peter the Great; defigns conformable to the character of the Emprefs.

Her troops, in purfuit of the Polifh confederates at Bar, did not pay more refpect to the Ottoman, than to the territories of Poland; they pillaged the city of Balta, in Moldavia. Upon demands of reparation, the Ruffians replied by a repetition of the fame outrages, in various parts of the Turkifh dominions, which were the afylum of the Poles. This was a violation of treaties, and of the

the laws of nations; the treaty of Pruth forbid that military tyranny which they exercised in Poland; as soon as the vigilant and enlighted policy of the Duke de Choiseul had decided the opinion of the Porte, or, as they themselves had been roused by the infractions of the treaties of Carlowitz, of Pruth, and of Constantinople, her declaration of war was confined to the necessity of guarding her frontiers. Having guarranteed the republic of Poland in the entire possession of her dminions, she was interested to prevent her

dismem-

dismemberment. Would to Heaven that other European courts had the same respect for, and the same firmness and courage to maintain their engagements.

Fortune, however, seconded injustice; the boldness and brutal, but firm, courage of her soldiers, gave advantages to the Russians, in spite of the inexperience and awkwardness of her officers. The valour of the Turks became ineffectual, by the continual change of their commanders, by the whimsical projects of some of their officers,

ficers, which counteracted general syftems; and the want of subordination, worfe even than cowardice in an army; by that corruption of the enemy which pervaded the Divan, and by that pufillanimity which was the affociate of Muftapha the Third upon the Turkifh throne.

After feveral defeats, the Porte figned, in 1774, the treaty of Kainardick, a monument of her weaknefs, an indication of her fupinenefs, and the herald of future misfortunes. This was the bafe base upon which Russia raised the superstructure of future designs; this was the instrument with which, as the clearsighted foresaw, the Empress would break that sceptre which she had intended to depress: from this period Europe, alarmed, or exaggerating the declamations of the parasites of the Empress, considered the Ottoman Empire at the eve of destruction.

This opinion was formed by vulgar minds, who have sufficient understanding to connect causes and

and effects, without any allowances for the changes wrought by chance, and by circumstances in human affairs, to confound necessity with accident, and bring political systems into the compass of conjecture and imagination.

But men, whom these idle speculations did not influence, saw Russia in a situation not less exhausted and enfeebled than her enemies: from the confession of Mareschal Munich himself, the last war but one, with Turky, had cost Russia two hundred and fifty

fifty thousand men;—imagination is amazed at the number of her soldiers which perished in Poland, in Tartary, on the Niester, on the Danube, and in the Archipelago, from 1768 to 1774. Pugatscheff massacred one hundred thousand, the plague destroyed eight hundred thousand men: in 1771 four hundred thousand Calmucks, persecuted by Russia, emigrated into Assia: these losses were repeated in a desert, which counts only twenty inhabitants for a square of three miles; where all the soldiers are pressed; where
a sol-

a soldier is taken from a proportion of thirty-five inhabitants: some thousand Greeks, forced, or enticed from their country, by insidious promises, some foreign colonies, abortive almost in their birth, a collection of vagabonds and adventurers, who found their only refuge in Russia, could not compensate this destructive depopulation:—true it is, that swarms of Cossacks and Calmucks, tribes more barbarous than their names, could hardly be regretted; but to lose and to posess is a contradiction; nor would generations be be produced with the facility with which manifestos and tables of population are framed or forged in newspapers; it is also true, that usurpations in Poland, and conquests in Turkey increase the number of her slaves; but assuredly Russia cannot supply her losses and her depopulation, by the conquests of her neighbours.

The finances, public credit, the fleet, the magazines, all felt the general loss; ruinous schemes, paper money, profusely increased, announced the want of resources;
it

it was evident that the Empress, in the midst of her victories and bombast, had earnestly solicited peace through the mediation of Mr. Murray, the English Resident at Constantinople, and of Mr. De Zegelin, the Prussian Minister. It was well known that that brilliant expedition to the Archipelago, which astonished Europe, had only produced vast expence, devastation in Greece, a victory due to English Experience, to the abilities of Elphinstone, Dugdale, and the Piemontese Count Mafin; but no conquests

quests were retained, no advantage, equal to the expence: prodigality of public money was accompanied with private waste, with magnificence, with largesses almost incredible: the empire, thus decorated with dazzling splendour, could scarcely depend upon two fifths of the revenues of England; and her circulation, her commerce, or her public riches, were far from sustaining these amazing enterprizes.

The campaign of 1774 was preceded by sickness and desertion

tion in the exhausted army of Romanzoff, who was saved by the timidity of the Grand Vizir, and his want of knowledge to profit by his advantages. An adventurer, a Cossack, had propagated the spirit of revolt, which had penetrated as far as Moscow, and proved the danger to which a bold man, less cruel, and more sagacious, might reduce an empire in the season of foreign warfare.

From all these observations, penetrating politicians foresaw, that

that in the intoxication of victory, Ruſſia knew no bounds; but that the exceſs of her proſperity would produce a limitation.

After the peace of Kainargik, the deſigns of diſmembering the Ottoman empire were diſcloſed. The Empreſs, exalted by her favourites, by writers, who excited her enthuſiaſm to emancipate Greece, and to reign at Conſtantinople, perceiving the delicacy of her ſituation, and informed of the revolutions which had dethroned ſo many of her predeceſſors.

fors, imagined fhe could elevate her reputation, and build her security upon the foundations of a new empire at the Bofphorus. Allegorical prints, engraved at Peterfburg, reprefented this Princefs trampling upon the ftandard of Mahomet, and repairing the ruins of Greece. Medals were ftruck with the reprefentation of the Labarum* :—all the arts, and all the talents of Ruffia, excited this idolatry, and ftimulated the

* The Standard of Conftantine, adopted by the Turks, was thus called.

defign

design of the destruction of the Ottoman empire in Europe. Partitioning treaties were the offspring of legions of mercenary writers.

By the treaty of Kainargik, the two powers had acknowledged the Crimea to be *free and independent*; they reciprocally engaged not to enter into any intrigues, nor any projects, to interrupt the mutual harmony; but the Court of Petersburg emulated the example of the Roman emperors, who sent generals into Gaul, or into Armenia,

menia, to proclaim their manifestos by the sound of the trumpet. Poland exhausted, could not oppose her decrees; in subtracting or misleading the Tartars from their dependence upon the Porte, they contrived to keep them in their own subordination—they acquired harbours and fortresses on the Euxine—a Khan, devoted to their interests, governed those regions, so famous in the dreams of mythology—arsenals, docks, and fortifications, were erected upon these frontiers, with batteries and citadels. This Imperial Colossus placed

placed one foot on Cherson, and the other in Kamschatka. Sahim Gueray, a docile chieftain, overlooked the nets with which he was encircled—gratitude and interest attached him to the Empress; his election was forced, like that of Poland, with the same views, and the same intentions.

This chief, the avowed partizan of Russia, who had sacrificed the national interests to the ambition of the Czarina, excited general discontent. In 1777 he was deprived of his military command,

mand, and thirty thousand indignant Tartars chose a successor. Neither his rights nor his powers, secured under a Russian guarranty, could keep him within neutral bounds; his troops advanced to pacify the Crimea, as they had heretofore pacified Poland. This district, declared independent by a treaty, attested in the most solemn manner, was attacked by a Russian army, who restord the Khan who had been dispossessed. His competitor sought an asylum at Constantinople, solicited succours, and offered to the Porte that

that appendage which she had lost. The example of Russia would have encouraged the Grand Seignior to interfere in this dispute, and to protect a chief freely and legally elected: but the faith of treaties, and the dictates of prudence, restrained the Divan; they refused an audience to the Tartar deputies, and they confined themselves to representations. But though the Russians remained masters of the country, and kept their acquisitions, the Porte had the weakness to acquiesce in the re-establishment of a chief protected by the Empress.

These pacific views, this imprudent concession, emboldened Russia; at the same instant she started new difficulties, and proposed a treaty of commerce, the principles of which revealed her intentions. Though this treaty was the disgrace of the empire, and though an insurrection had put Constantinople in danger, the same councils, the same inconsiderate moderation governed Turkey; and in 1779, she signed an additional

additional convention presented to her as the seal of an eternal reconciliation.

These sacrifices, it was easy to foretel, would produce no more than a momentary truce, and that new disputes would spring from this source. That policy must be condemned which avoids a war by those concessions which assure to adversaries a still greater facility of hostile operations.

The Porte had a new danger to encounter, while the Empress had hopes of a new ally. Whether it was the effect of an inconstancy peculiar to the cabinet of Petersburg, or by the operation of some connections with the House of Austria, her treaty with the King of Prussia had expired. The court of Vienna had forgot her old fears and her ancient principles; eight years before, she would not suffer the Russians to extend their influence in Moldavia, nor allow them to approach her frontiers, nor pass the Danube

nube and give laws to Turkey. The Empress Queen, and Prince Kaunitz, influenced by these maxims, entered into a negotiation with the Porte*: but the death of Maria-Theresa introduced new systems; distrust was changed into reciprocal confidence. Before this period, the peace of Teschen had been concluded under the mediation of Catherine the Second. A mysterious inter-

---

* The King of Prussia's Memoirs relate the alarm created in the court of Vienna, by the ambition of Russia at this time.

view

view between that Princess and the Emperor had taken place, which had united interests so apparently discordant. A secret treaty confirmed the fears of Europe, and engaged the general attention touching those projects upon which this formidable association was grounded. Such was the crisis in which the Empress, in 1782, invaded the Crimea.

Sahim Gueray, the mercenary and felonious instrument of the Russian policy, abdicated his dignity: but did he surrender it to his

his constituents? No; he sold it to the Empress: he sold that sovereignty to which he had no claim. This elected chief sold his masters and his electors; but this cession was ridiculous. If the King of Poland had sold his throne, would the rest of Europe ratify the bargain? Immediately a Russian army plundered those provinces which were rendered free in 1777, subjected them to her laws, and an apologising manifesto followed the invasion.

When

When Tamerlane, Attila, and Nadir Shaw, subjected their neighbours, equity was a slight obstacle; without scruples, and without chicane, they exercised their powers; nor did shame colour or masque their injustice. In our days we are told, that politeness, humanity, and philosophy, violate treaties, dismember states, spread discord, and legitimate usurpations. Poland abuses her liberty: slavery, it is said, should relieve her from anarchy. Are dissentions excited in Sweden, publick liberty becomes the pretext.

text.—Ignorant countries, like the Crimea, should be polished by force of arms.

In her apologising manifesto, the Empress announced, that she had lost the product of her victories, if Sahim Gueray did not remain under her protection:— that was to say, that she had consecrated the independence of the Tartars, and the freedom of their elections, so long as those franchises were subservient to her interests. By a parity of reason, the Porte could usurp the sovereign authority of this diſtrict; thus the independence of the Crimea, unconditionally eſtabliſhed in 1774, conſiſted in receiving the law from either of thoſe powers, whenever one of them ſhould deem it expedient to diſpoſe of her ſovereignty. According to this manifeſto, it was the love of order and public tranquillity, which, with the Divine aſſiſtance, had introduced the Ruſſian arms into the Crimea; which had exerciſed a tyrannical ſway, diſpoſed of the ſovereignty, appeaſed revolts,

revolts, and given a supremacy over the sovereign himself.

All these measures were *dictated solely* by the imperial regard for *humanity*, grounded upon a *conviction*, that Tartars could not appreciate the *value* of *independence*. Lastly, by the right of ancient *conquest*, which had been annihilated by the treaty of 1774, and by the only method of ensuring the blessings of a *lasting* and permanent peace.

By the extension of such arguments, the Czarina had a right to the possession of Turkey. The *ennui* of debates, the care of tranquillity, the security of good neighbourhood, would have given similar possessory claims to Russia in the surrounding provinces. Georgia, Moldavia, as well as the Crimea, would furnish subjects of mutual discord. Step by step, this progressive argument would reach Egypt, and every province connected with, and tributary to, the Porte, which might, from those circumstances,

create

create alarms and inquietudes; so that, from a chain of reasoning, it might be ultimately, and justly, inferred, that nothing but the universal subjection of Turkey could ensure a solid and permanent pacification.

Upon the intelligence of this enterprize, the Porte, suspended between surprise and indignation, prepared a formidable resistance—If a patriotic policy had had its due influence, she would have reguarded her safety, her just resentment, and popular tumults;

she would have rigged her squadrons and struck her tents—a powerful influence, prescribed by moderation at least, delayed those enterprizes which true policy enjoined: doubts of disasters were artfully infused, the operations of the Emperor were magnified, the auxiliary of Russia ready to act in concert with a hundred thousand men. These temporising councils prevailed over motives of self-defence; and although Constantinople, taken in forty-nine days, by Mahomet the Second, had remained defenceless since

since that period, and without any barrier towards the Black Sea, a convention signed in January 1784, authorised the usurpation of the Crimea and of Couban, but upon articles which were infringed with the same facility with which they had been framed.

Georgia and Cabartas soon afterwards experienced the same fate; the Prince Heraclius was bribed; Egypt was inflamed by the intrigues of Russia: everywhere, particularly in Moldavia and Wallachia, in the Archipelago, go, her confuls were incendiaries employed to corrupt the vaffals of the Porte, and to excite infurrections. Since the treaty of 1774, two of thofe emiffaries had been punifhed, and the Emprefs regarded their punifhment as an infraction of the laws of nations. In the midft of peace, fome Greeks were taken away by force; if Ruffian fhips entered the Propontis, it was by falfe reprefentations of the number and tonnage of thofe veffels; every day gave rife to fome vexatious pretenfions, and they proceeded to enter

enter into the secret councils of the Divan, to interfere in her administration, to influence the choice, and to exact the dismission of public officers.

The observer of these differences, so difficult to terminate, after multiplied treaties and conventions, must necessarily ask what would be the issue of this war of increasing grievances and conventions, each of which has generated new encroachments and new troubles? The demands of Russia increased in proportion to the

the condescension or hesitation of the Divan. The opinions of Europe were divided upon the consequences of this crisis, when she saw the second Catherine realise the fable of Sesostris, departing with inconvenient pomp from the frozen plains of Ingria, to display her powers on the embouchures of the rivers on the Black Sea, to penetrate into new conquests desolated since their submission, with a dazzling and imposing procession; and received on the banks of the Nieper by a King of Poland, in the Tauride by the Emperor of Germany,

Germany, and marching with a convoy of forty thousand men, to take possession of a Mussulman country, under the eyes of the successor of the Khaliphs. While this Princess displayed an Oriental magnificence before a people, whom, in her last manifesto, she had called an asylum of freebooters —while the Greek description of the road to Bizantium appeared upon the gateway at Cherson; she disquieted the Turks by new diplomatic hostilities.

This

This pageant, this oftentation, at length roufed the lion from his flumber. The Emprefs was fcarcely returned to Peterfburg, before her envoy was imprifoned in the feven towers, the Black Sea was covered with fhips, the Turkifh troops were marching through a territory, which had recently re-echoed her triumphal acclamations.

Political events, and the filent revolutions which were fecretly operating in many parts of Europe, feemed to favour a refolution,

tion, which was juſt and deciſive. Moſt cabinets were tired of the Ruſſian haughtineſs, or diſturbed by her projects; and her intimacy with Auſtria could not leſſen this anxiety. Penetration could not reject the ſurmiſe, that a ſecret jealouſy ſubſiſted between the two courts, and that the Emperor, an enlightened prince, having the choice of vicinity, would prefer the exhauſted Turks in his alliances, to the Ruſſians, whoſe preponderance was every where converted into a ſovereign influence. Since the peace of Belgrade, the

the good intelligence between Vienna and the Porte, was not interrupted. The Turks respected the misfortunes of Maria Theresa; nor did they profit by the embarrassments of 1740, nor those of the seven-years war.—Some light clouds were seen to interrupt this harmony:—the Divan had dispersed them with moderation: the Bosnian limits were amicably arranged, and the districts of Buckovine were ceded by Turkey with unexpected facility.

From

From these circumstances it was supposed that the court of Vienna would act, at least, the part of a simple auxiliary, if she did not represent the character of a dignified neutrality.

Though the principal, and oldest, ally of Turkey was occupied by internal troubles, indecisive in her political system, and could only relieve her by negociations, many other states offered secret services. The Empress had cooled the attachment of England by a conduct, which in London was called

called ingratitude. Detached from Pruffia, she had promised her guarrantee for the Bavarian exchange; and Berlin confidered the court of Peterfburg as the Emperor's affociate. Poland, meditating revenge, confidered the Turks as their guardians; and laftly, Sweden had equal interefts to defend, to render her guarantee, fo often flighted, refpectable, and to refume, after twenty years interval, her equilibre in the North.

CHAP.

CHAP. VIII.

Constitution—Russian Influence in Sweden—Affairs of Finland.

THIS state was the most aggrieved by Russia; the power which deprived her of so many provinces in the beginning, governed her by a corrupt and despotic influence in the sequel of this century. The conduct of Charles the Twelfth, the pride, and the misfortune of Sweden, had

had produced a revolution in the government, in which the paſt only was conſidered, without any regard to future evils. Experience of evils often affects nations too much to allow them to weigh and to examine their remedial proviſions, the inconveniencies of which are often long concealed, till futurity diſcovers their fatal conſequences.

The impetuous diſcontent of Sweden, or of ſome demagogues, deſtroyed the balance of the component parts of her conſtitution.

In

In the recefs of her diets, the power lodged in the fenate controlled the royal authority; the nomination and qualification of fenators were given, with the whole legiflative power, to the ftates. The executive power was fubjected to a body, each member of which might be difmiffed by the ftates; and the judicial power was vefted in their committees. During their feffions, the complete executive power was vefted in a fecret commiffion of the ftates, without limit or balance, in a body of feven, perhaps eight,

eight, hundred men: The royal authority was confined to mere representation; the King could not dismiss an impertinent servant; and, in Mr. Sheridan's words, " he appeared only as a " state pageant, decorated for ho- " lidays and courtly festivals*."

This

* Mr. Sheridan (the son of the late Manager of the Dublin theatre, who has exemplified his theory in the education of his children, and to whose valuable labours the translator is happy to advert) was secretary to Sir John Goodrick, when the revolution, which he has recorded, took place in 1774. He was afterwards Secretary

This conſtitution favoured all the defects, all the diſorders of internal policy, and all the ſchemes of foreign adverſaries; and conſequently, by the treaty of Newſtadt, in 1721, the Czar became its guarantee.

Experience is the ſureſt teſt of government: principles may be

tary at War in Ireland, but he was diſmiſſed in 1789, after the great queſtion of the Regency was decided, with a penſion of 800l. The appointment of his ſucceſſor was ſo oddly contrived, as to loſe, inſtead of acquiring parliamentary influence in Ireland.

condemned when attended with pernicious effects. What was the portrait of Sweden in 1772? General weakness, shameful neglect in all her departments; an inconsiderate war in 1757, unskillfully, dishonourably conducted; the love of glory subdued by the spirit of intrigue, and the welfare of the state by a criminal selfishness: places conferred, and powers torn from their monarch by a faction; all was venal; each suffrage, and each majority, the objects of mercantile calculation. "Corruption was so transcen- "dant,"

"dant," says Frederick the Great, "that at one time a French, and at another a Russian, faction prevailed, while the national party never predominated."

Russia played the principal part in this scene of confusion; meditating the arbitration of the Swedish government, no opportunity was lost to profit by the general anarchy; and her fancy decided, in 1750, the contested bounds of Finland.

Ruffia, allied with France and Auftria, from the diflike of Elizabeth to the King of Pruffia, produced that demolition in 1756 of the feeble remnant of royal authority, as the firft fruits of that combination, accompanied with mortifying infults to the King and Queen: and laftly, that war in 1756, where Sweden followed as a vaffal in proceffion, without intereft, reafon, or juftice, and faw her brave legions facrificed to the frivolity of her government.

Intrigues and bribes at Stockholm were doubled since the accession of the second Catherine: the predominance of the party of the Bonnets was secured; she dictated all their resolutions; and while she laboured to introduce anarchy into Poland, she confirmed and ratified it in Sweden. Nothing remained except the dethronement of the King; when the intrepidity of Gustavus the Third prevented this last attempt, restored the empire of the laws, circumscribed that liberty which consisted only in the sale of public welfare, and banished for ever that despotism of corruption under which she had so long been afflicted.

The Empress had engaged the King of Prussia in a convention, to guaranty the Swedish government as established by the treaty of Newstadt in 1721. From thence we may estimate her surprise at this revolution.—" An-" ger and vengeance," says Frederick the Second, " would have " had an immediate operation, " had not the Turks firmly resisted

" fifted the hard and imperious
" terms of peace which fhe had
" propofed......'. The King of
" Sweden, aware of the danger
" by which he was menaced,
" laboured a conciliation with
" Denmark, that he might be
" engaged with a fingle adver-
" fary."

Here we have the moft revered, and the moft decifive evidence of the defigns of the Emprefs againft Sweden: after this, it is no lefs true than it is aftonifhing, that in a reply, contained in a libel,

bel; avowed by the cabinet of Peterſburg, entitled, "*Obſerva-tions and Hiſtorical Ecclairciſſe-ments*," ſtudiouſly circulated in Finland, effrontery could miſrepreſent theſe precautions of Guſtavus, againſt the joint animoſity of Denmark and Ruſſia, under the idea of a voluntary and fanciful aggreſſion, which the leaſt menace from Ruſſia would have prevented.

Aſſuredly Ruſſia was not then in a formidable ſtate — Had the King of Sweden profited by her loſſes,

losses, the absence, sickness, and misery of her troops, the terror and indications of revolt, upon the near approach of Pugatscheff, he had nothing to fear; save only an abusive and sophistical manifesto from the Russian ministers.

This Prince was governed by other maxims: he saved the Empress from new dangers; and public notoriety will prove a chain of solicitude, to maintain harmony and good understanding between the two courts.

Notwith-

Notwithstanding this determination, the Russian intrigues increased, the slightest pretexts for discontent were magnified in Sweden by misrepresentation; emissaries were found in her provinces, to inflame the people by false insinuations.

Since the peace of Abo, Russia had secretly laboured to detach Finland from Sweden: beside this enterprize, dictated by her ruling principle of usurpation, the vast projects of the Czarina induced her to prevent the efforts of of Sweden to affift her ally, and to attack Ruffia in a vulnerable place. At one time, fhe fomented the fpirit of revolt, at another, fhe promifed the Finlanders independency. The Baron Sprengporten, loaded with the favours of the King of Sweden, and invefted with great employments in Finland, with every mark of confidence and bounty, was gained by the offers of the Emprefs, and had no fcruples to betray his king, his country, and the moft facred obligations.

A Ruffian officer, under the pretext of curiofity, had, in 1786, vifited the pofts of Finland, reconnoitred thofe which might be attacked, and endeavoured to found and to corrupt the principles of the inhabitants.

This clandeftine war engaged the unceafing vigilance of the Swedifh King: of the fecret defigns of Ruffia he could not doubt; but the moment of open refiftance was not come; and danger was concealed, left the king-

kingdom should be involved in a premature rupture.

At length the Porte was roused from its lethargy.—To indicate the aggressor would be idle:—assuredly, tired with the hostilities of ten years, she was not obliged to attend the visit of the Russians at the gates of Constantinople.— Their treaty with Sweden, in 1759, enabled them to solicit succours.—The interest and engagements of Gustavus concurred with their desire.

Russia

Russia immediately resolved to cripple Sweden, by those measures which had ruined Poland, enslaved the Crimea, and subjected Courland. The embers of the flame in 1772 were revived—the Count Rosamouski resumed the part of his predecessors as minister of the Empress—every engine was employed to excite a faction against the King—the Russian Envoy's conduct was most indiscreet—public seduction was evident in his words and actions—in the capital, and under the King's eyes, no Ambassador ever braved

braved so audaciously the respect due to sovereigns, the rights of hospitality, and the duties of his function. The Count Rosamouski had forgot discretion; his declarations were outrages, appeals to the people against their sovereign:—bold and insidious, these hostile notes infused rancor and gall into the hearts of too many. —The government did not forget in this conjuncture what was due to public tranquillity and the laws of nations.—The king declined to acknowledge his powers as a minister, and compelled him to abandon

abandon the theatre of his intrigues.

The Empress not only justified, but complained of the dismission of her minister:—Europe was shocked at the conduct of the court of Petersburg, which treated self-defence as a proof of hostility.—Neither respect for kings, nor prudence, nor conciliation, formed any part of her conduct; even peace was announced with insulting language.

When

When victory had abandoned her arms, artifice succeeded; her agents tampered with the officers of the Finland troops—the most despotic court in the universe resounded the word liberty in the ears of the Swedish subjects: some of whom forgot their allegiance to their King and country, deserted them in the hour of danger, and entered into a traiterous correspondence.— A terrible example, an awful lesson, for those states whose destiny placed their interests in opposition to the designs of Russia.

CHAP. IX.

Negotiations of England and Prussia with the Czarina — Interests of the Maritime Powers — The Importance of the Establishment of Russia, as a Naval Power, in the Mediterranean.

THE inflexible pride of that court prevailed at the moment of the bursting of a storm; when Poland was ready to break her chains, and Prussia to second her laudable designs; when the cabinets

nets of Potsdam and of London engaged in the same interest: all mediation was scornfully rejected; she received the offer of the Swedish King, to reconcile her to the Porte, with disdain; which compelled him to the necessity of defensive measures, and the completion of his engagements with Turkey.

The mediation of England was equally rejected without regard to their alliance, to past service, or the slight ties by which they were allied. The English pride and

and liberality were ſhocked with ſtratagems, with diſdain, with hoſtile intimations, from a court which owed her eternal obligations. The expedition to the Archipelago was ſolely to be aſcribed to Engliſh aid and aſſiſtance, and to them the glory of it ſhould be aſcribed: the diſabled fleet of the Empreſs harboured, repaired, and victualled by England, could never have cleared the Channel without the ſkill of Britiſh pilots; nor would they have burned the Turkiſh fleet, had it not been for the ability of the firſt of the maritime

ritime powers. If England enabled the Ruſſian flag to appear without diſhonour before the Dardanelles, and zealouſly befriended her negotiations, what was her acknowledgement? A deſertion when England was almoſt overpowered by her enemies, that armed neutrality which deprived them of thoſe mariners they procured from the Baltic, which enabled Holland to carry on an illicit trade, which ſpeciouſly gave the title of the protectreſs of marine freedom to the Empreſs, but which, in reality, was a mortal wound

wound to the importance of England.

The English capitals and traders are the great resource of the Russian commerce, the vital principles of her tardy circulation; though the balance of trade is a loss of near one million annually to England, though English ships constitute the half of the vessels which arrive annually at Cronstadt, the Empress has procrastinated the renewal of their commercial treaty:—eluding the solicita-

solicitations of the English cabinet, promising much and terminating nothing, the negotiation has languished, and the effects of their projected arrangements are as humiliating as they are ridiculous.

The new allies of England invited the Empress to reflect upon the proposed joint arbitration of Great Britain and Prussia. The successor of Frederick the Great, ambitious more of the title of a peacemaker than of a conqueror, held the balance with a firm and impartial

impartial hand, and propoſed an amicable adjuſtment.—His reign daily acquired, without the eclat of war, that reputation, which wiſe and able meaſures, the wiſdom of councils, the moderation and juſt management of power, never fail to beſtow. The King of Pruſſia had diſcovered a mine of miſchief formed in Poland, by Ruſſian emiſſaries, equally dangerous to Pruſſia, as well as to Turkey.—An excluſive alliance, was projected between that republic and Ruſſia; by the energy of his declarations, and the conviction

viction of his resolution, the court of Berlin warded off this stroke, and gave new life to Poland. Whether the Russian ministers were blinded by the facility and possibility of a great event, or whether Catherine, intoxicated by success, consulted more her favourites than her interest, she rejected, with disdain, the idea of mediation; she braved all risques, and the moderation of the King of Prussia solely prevented a formidable alliance of five powers against Russia.

CHAP.

CHAP. X.

Conclusion — General Remarks — Summary of this Work *.

SUCH are the hiftorical features of the prefent time, of which all Europe is a witnefs. Her Kings have viewed perhaps with too

---

* This conclufive chapter is, perhaps, the moft valuable part of this work. A fhort and comprehenfive account of the political interefts of the different ftates in Europe

too much prudence, the progress of this enterprising policy, by which the laws of nations have been

rope is much wanted: and it is very extraordinary, that, at the present crisis, an able pamphlet has not appeared upon Continental affairs, nor upon the part which this country might act as the arbiter of Europe.

According to what, I believe, may be considered as the most authentic compilation of parliamentary debates, before they were regularly published in newspapers, in 1773-4, I mean the debates in the Lilliputian club, where the names of the principal speakers are travestied been annulled, the faith of treaties has difappeared, and the abufe of power has legitimated ufurpation. This

tied in the Gentleman's Magazine; the principal debates in the days of Sir Robert Walpole turned upon foreign treaties and Continental interefts.

This Chapter refembles that fhort, but excellent, abridgement of the ftate of Europe, by Sir William Temple, in 1673, prefented to the Duke of Ormond by that great man at the end of his fecond embaffy, in anfwer to his fhort queftion, " What was neceffary to be done?"— or what part this country fhould take at that crifis

It

This vast empire, which, for twenty years, has spread terror, corruption, despotism, and war, embraces

It were much to be desired that some able man, in the diplomatic line, would favour the public with some chart of the present schemes, alliances, connections, and interests, of the Continent—I say the public, because, notwithstanding some new doctrines, publicity is the vital principle of a free country; information and intelligence can alone animate their exertions, and direct their energy. It is very easy to talk of committing lives and fortunes; but mankind must be persuaded that they are in the right, before they can be prevailed upon to engage
with

embraces all varieties of climate, and comprehends every species of resource. Seas inaccessible to European

with zeal and patriotism in foreign wars: blinfolded exertions are childish and contemptible.

For such a character as Sir William Temple, we shall look in vain, while our embassies are bestowed merely from parliamentary interest, or rendered commodious for men who cannot live conveniently at home. This great man was patronized by the Duke of Ormond, in consequence of his exertions in the Irish parliament after the restoration, where, as representative of the county of Carlow, he ropean fleets; deserts or enslaved countries are her frontiers: hitherto, impressions upon her territory

he appeared as the first speaker, and the ablest member, of that assembly. Some time ago I was much disappointed in my application to the nobleman who inherits his name and virtues, for some early memorials of Sir William Temple, as this part of his life has not been dwelt upon by any of his biographers; and these anecdotes to which I allude, were collected, with some materials, for a parliamentary history of Ireland to the revolution, in which I have been for some time engaged. This work I intend to form upon Mr. Hatsell's plan, and to render it entertaining ritory have been haſtily deemed impracticable. While her adverſaries remain upon the defenſive, ſwarms of undiſciplined ſavages emigrate from their habitations, and deſtroy extenſive countries in a campaign. Pruſſia and Poland ſtill bleed from thoſe

taining by ſome memoirs of the Duke of Ormond, from papers communicated to me by a particular friend, the heir of that illuſtrious nobleman, to whom I have the honour of being nearly allied: and I ſhall leave it to my country, if I may hope that a ſufficient period is allotted to me to accompliſh ſo laborious an undertaking.

ravages,

ravages, when troops which are mowed down without being subdued, are animated by pillage, by fanaticifm, or by the ambition of their fovereign, who in lofing foldiers, only lofes flaves ; — woe to thofe ftates which border upon this deftructive power!

Peace muft be purchafed by facrifices, or fecured by a preparation commenfurate to the danger. Ruffia menaces at the fame time, Turkey, the North, and Germany: the reduction of one, would accelerate the conqueft of the others. Solitary refiftance is vain, againft an empire which can produce foldiers, like grains of fand, whofe policy has no other principles than thofe of intereft, and whofe bold maxims correfpond with that fortune, which has fo long favoured their projects.

By the fchemes fhe has executed in Poland, that republic; and Courland, are warned of the danger which threatens them, if they fhould not ferioufly advert to timely provifions for their fafety.

Before

Before the Ruffian was united with the Auftrian army, Frederick the Great was furprifed at the rapidity of their progrefs; he had feen them penetrate into the heart of his ftates, and lay Pruffia under contribution, a country always expofed to invafion, while Poland and Courland are under Ruffian influence. Ruffia, as the auxiliary of the chief of the German empire, and affociated in his projects, can attack Pruffia on the fouth as well as the north, aid the Emperor by her diverfions, and menace the liberty of Germany.

Sweden maintains her situation, thanks to the firmness and precaution of her king; but recent events reveal the secret of that slender thread upon which her tranquillity depends, and demonstrates the necessity of a balance which may place the Empress in due bounds of limitation.

A similar interest should affect the politics of Denmark, if the memory of their absurd rivality with

with Sweden, and the prejudices of her ministers, should no longer fascinate that country. Can she not perceive that her alliance is an instrument which she lends to Russia to disquiet her neighbours, and to tyrannize over the North? Is it not clear, that in lending her influence to weaken, or to crush the powers on the Baltic, she will ultimately contribute to her own depression? What would be her security, if the neighbouring powers should be disabled, or subdued by Russia? Every thing conspires to induce

Denmark to a mutual defensive alliance, to maintain the equilibre, to counterbalance the preponderance of Ruffia, to imitate that noble fyftem, the Germanic league, the rampart of weak ftates againft the power of a great empire.

The maritime and commercial ftates, the South, Italy, and Venice, in particular, are affected by the fame interefts, and fhould participate in the fame apprehenfions. Should Ruffia eftablifh her power in the Mediterranean, human

man foresight cannot appreciate or comprehend the wide and vast effects of such a revolution.

To all these, I shall subjoin the supereminent consideration of the happiness of Russia herself, of her true glory, of her national interests, sacrificed to the eclat of a transitory reign, whose trophies are stained with blood. That nation, which has surprised Europe with the rapidity of her civilization, should endeavour to consummate that great work; to which peace is essential. The
natural

natural aptitude of that robuſt, flexible, and penetrating people, to repair the ravages of ſucceſſive wars, would facilitate this deſign. They yet want arts, manufactures, internal and foreign commerce, capitals, population; and her civilization does not extend beyond Moſcow. This cannot be the work of a ſovereign, engroſſed with ideas of territorial aggrandizement; nor of favourites trembling at her nod, at their future deſtiny, and providing aſylums in the neighbouring ſtates as refuges from deſpotiſm. This great

great donation is reserved to the nobility, to the nation itself, formed to give examples of virtue, which decorate humanity. It is alone by exerting her activity in the centre of the state, that her wounds can be healed, and that she can support the inconvenient and gigantic extent of her empire.

The Russians still proudly remember that Prince who, unintentionally perhaps, prepared them for freedom, while they were civilized as slaves. Of all the plans and schemes of that great man, the

the most admirable, though the least noticed, was that of abandoning two thirds of that vast empire to bears and to nature, to concenter the whole population in the provinces which are within a practicable distance of the capital, and to strengthen his country by consolidation. This policy is a satire upon the present reign; a policy assuredly adopted by the intelligent part of the community; they have too much good sense not to lament, that all her powers have been turned against her genius and disposition,

against

against her interest, and to see the destruction of her resources, without the acquisition of any solid advantage. Of what moment are vain and pompous conquests, which exist only in sounds, in hymns, in Te Deums, and in festivals?*

May

* This sentence has been extended by the Translator—no other liberty has been taken in this English version, save only that of dividing it into Chapters, and adding a few notes. This Work has been authenticated to me, as the work of the King of Sweden, though it cannot be supposed that it was compiled without assistance

May the succeffor to this throne, that Prince, whom Europe has obferved in his travels, accompanied with fuch modefty, an exaffiftance, as the Pofthumous Works of Frederick the Great were revifed by the Pruffian Minifter, Count Hertzberg. No pains have been fpared to make the tranflation and the printing as accurate as poffible. It is to be hoped the Public will accept of apologies for any miftake in a work undertaken in a period of indifpofition, and of political turbulence; which could not (the Public muft fuppofe) be accompanied with pleafant reflections, nor be altogether favourable to the literary purfuits of the Tranflator.

ample of private virtues, and whose benign inclinations may heal the wounds of those fruitless wars. May the Grand Duke be no longer guided by this absurd, and romantic policy. May he substitute in the place of fallacious grandeur, that true greatness which results from the moderation of princes, and from the prosperity of their people.

FINIS.

www.ingramcontent.com/pod-product-compliance
Lightning Source LLC
Chambersburg PA
CBHW032121230426
43672CB00009B/1812